WORLD OF KNOWLEDGE

The Evolution
of Life

David John

Richard Moody

Macdonald/Silver Burdett

Editorial Manager	Judith Maxwell
Senior Editor	Lynne Williams
Editors	Brenda Clarke
	Bridget Daly
Series Designers	QED (Alastair Campbell
	and Edward Kinsey)
Series Consultant	Keith Lye
Production	John Moulder
Picture Research	Jenny De Gex

© Macdonald Educational Ltd. 1980
First published 1980
Macdonald Educational Ltd.
Holywell House,
Worship Street,
London EC2A 2EN

Published in the
United States by
Silver Burdett Company
Morristown, N.J.
1980 Printing
ISBN 0 382 06511 5

PRINTED IN ITALY.

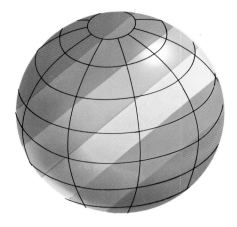

World of Knowledge

This book breaks new ground in the method it uses to present information to the reader. The unique page design combines narrative with an alphabetical reference section and it uses colourful photographs, diagrams and illustrations to provide an instant and detailed understanding of the book's theme. The main body of information is presented in a series of chapters that cover, in depth, the subject of this book. At the bottom of each page is a reference section which gives, in alphabetical order, concise articles which define, or enlarge on, the topics discussed in the chapter. Throughout the book, the use of SMALL CAPITALS in the text directs the reader to further information that is printed in the reference section. The same method is used to cross-reference entries within each reference section. Finally, there is a comprehensive index at the end of the book that will help the reader find information in the text, illustrations and reference sections. The quality of the text, and the originality of its presentation, ensure that this book can be read both for enjoyment and for the most up-to-date information on the subject.

Contents

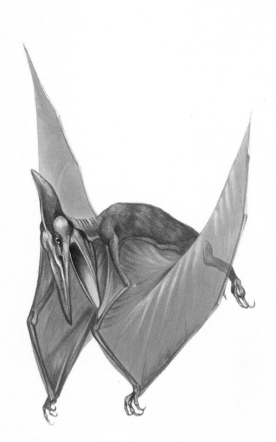

Introduction

Every living thing on the Earth today has a history stretching back over millions of years, and the changes which have taken place within that time are described in **The Evolution of Life.** Although the mystery of life's origins on Earth has not yet been solved, scientists are discovering more and more about the early Earth from its rocks and from the fossils they contain. These reveal an overwhelming diversity of life forms in our world — from simple, single cells to huge trees and enormous dinosaurs. Some of these forms are remarkably similar to plants and animals alive today. Others have died out, leaving only their remains behind. **The Evolution of Life** also traces the course of life among individuals, explaining how one generation passes its hereditary characteristics to its offspring, and how plants and animals adapt successfully, by 'selection', to the surroundings in which they live.

Our knowledge of the chemistry of life, and the discovery of fossils in some of the
world's oldest rocks, help us to understand how life may first have appeared and spread
on the primeval Earth.

The Origins of Life

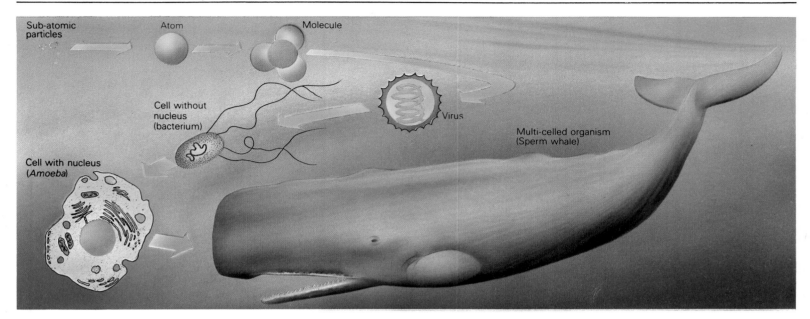

Sub-atomic particles · Atom · Molecule · Cell without nucleus (bacterium) · Virus · Cell with nucleus (*Amoeba*) · Multi-celled organism (Sperm whale)

Because there are obvious differences between an animal or plant and, say, a rock, many people assume that the difference between life and non-life is as easy to describe. In fact the ancient Greek philosopher Aristotle (384–322 BC) was nearer to the truth when he noted that on a scale from the smallest ATOMS to complex organisms it is hard to answer the question: what is life? Growth, reproduction and respiration (*see page 6*) could be listed as some of its properties, yet these are also known in the non-living state. On the other hand, VIRUSES, which are on the threshold of life, may show none of the three properties mentioned. It is perhaps more sensible, then, to see life as a property of matter when it reaches a particular stage of complexity.

Life on Earth
Life comprises the most plentiful elements in the universe — hydrogen, carbon, nitrogen and oxygen. However, there has been disagreement over how these first combined into living beings. The ancient Greeks believed in spontaneous generation, thinking, for example, that frogs came into being from damp earth. This view was finally shown to be wrong in the 1800s by Louis PASTEUR, who demonstrated that living organisms, including BACTERIA, were created only as offspring of parent organisms. With Charles DARWIN'S ideas on evolution, his work led to the theory, now widely accepted, that life started on the primeval Earth in a warm 'soup' of ORGANIC MOLECULES. On the other hand, a very different idea was advanced by Svante ARRHENIUS. It stated that the Earth was seeded by life from other planets and that life itself is eternal. His 'PANSPERMIA' concept does not fit the observed facts, but some astronomers have recently presented a new case for the theory that life began beyond the Earth. Finally, there remains the explanation that life was created by a supernatural force, as in the story of Genesis.

Above: Many scientists believe that matter differs simply in its degree of organization, and that 'life' results when a particular level of organization is reached. So it is possible to progress from sub-atomic particles to increasingly more complex arrangements of matter — from the atom, molecule, virus, single-celled organisms without a nucleus, single-celled organisms with a nucleus, to multi-celled organisms like the mighty whale.

Reference

A **Aerobic** means with oxygen. Nearly all EUKARYOTES need oxygen to combine with the carbon in their food and so produce energy. Carbon dioxide and water are formed as waste products.
Amber is the fossilized resin of coniferous trees and is comparatively rare. As it oozed from trees the resin often trapped insects, and a large variety of these is known from amber of the

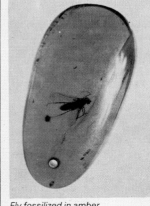
Fly fossilized in amber

Oligocene age. The insects' outer parts are perfectly preserved, but the soft internal tissues are missing.
Anaerobic means without oxygen. Some BACTERIA cannot reproduce or grow in the presence of oxygen — these are called obligate anaerobes. Facultative anaerobes can tolerate oxygen, but also live without it. Instead of combining the carbon in their food with oxygen, obligate anaerobes gain energy by breaking down carbon-rich substances such as glucose into simpler components. Energy

is released in the process.
Aragonite is one kind of crystalline calcium carbonate (the other is calcite). Aragonite is more unstable than calcite if exposed to air or fresh water. But both kinds are often destroyed by the action of water, especially in sandy rocks. The calcium carbonate parts of organisms are therefore often only preserved as CASTS, or are replaced by another mineral such as pyrites.
Arrhenius, Svante (1859–1927) was a Swedish chemist who first set out the theory of PANSPERMIA in a

number of popular books and scientific papers. According to this idea, organisms could have journeyed across space from another solar system, aided by the pressure of radiation — a sort of solar wind. In recent years variants of this theory have been put forward by several scientists.
Atoms are extremely small particles. They make up elements, the simplest components into which substances can be sub-divided. The atoms in any one element are identical, but those of different elements have

Above: This scene represents the Earth as it may have looked early in its history. Volcanic gases are generally believed to have created the Earth's atmosphere and oceans. Electrical discharges in this primitive atmosphere may have formed organic molecules which dissolved in the oceans. Such molecules are thought to have provided the raw materials from which life developed.

The first living organisms

The Earth is about 4,600 million years old, while the earliest known organisms are from rocks roughly 3,300 million years old. Assuming that life began on Earth, it must have started some time in the first 1,300 million years after the planet was formed. During this time the Earth's atmosphere and oceans were also created by huge outpourings of gases from its volcanoes. Judging from the gases emitted in volcanic eruptions today, the early atmosphere contained lots of hydrogen, ammonia and methane, and smaller amounts of carbon dioxide and nitrogen. The oxygen-nitrogen mixture we breathe today came much later, after plants evolved that were capable of PHOTOSYNTHESIS — a process in which oxygen is formed as a by-product. Without oxygen there would have been no OZONE layer in the upper atmosphere, as there is now, to filter out ULTRAVIOLET LIGHT from the Sun's rays. Therefore ultraviolet light, which is harmful to all living things, must have reached the Earth's surface. It was in this seemingly hostile setting that life is supposed to have started. The sequence of events may have been as follows.

Creation of life

Lightning flashes and ultraviolet light supplied enough energy for the relatively simple ingredients in the atmosphere to combine into more complex organic molecules. Some of these molecules are seen as the building blocks, or PRE-BIOTIC substances, from which life later developed. A similar effect has taken place in the laboratory by sending high-voltage sparks through mixtures of gases believed to resemble the Earth's primitive atmosphere. Several molecules produced in these experiments could be described as pre-biotic, since they are found in both PROTEIN and NUCLEIC ACIDS, the two essential components in every living organism. After pre-biotic substances formed in the atmosphere on the primeval Earth, they dissolved in the oceans, turning them into a thin soup.

different properties. Combinations of atoms are known as molecules. Oxygen and hydrogen are elements, while water is a molecule which is made up of 2 hydrogen atoms and 1 oxygen atom.
Autotrophs are organisms which can nourish themselves. They make their own food from simple non-living substances acquired from their surroundings. Green plants are the autotrophs most familiar to us. All animal life and fungi depend ultimately on autotrophs for their existence.

B **Bacteria** are the simplest living organisms, and consist of a single cell. They are minute — in fact it has been worked out that one thousand billion individuals (1,000,000,000,000) of a certain bacteria could be packed into one cubic centimetre. There is another group of single-celled organisms called Protista, which includes *Amoeba*, but they have a much more complex structure. Bacteria belong to the PROKARYOTES, whereas members of the protists are EUKARYOTES.
Blue-green algae closely

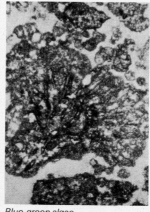

Blue-green algae

resemble BACTERIA (despite their name) and are otherwise known as cyanobacteria. They are made up from single cells or from cells joined end to end to form filaments. They may also be formed from colonies of individual cells or filaments held together in a jelly-like mass.

C **Cainozoic** is the name of the ERA which began at the end of Cretaceous times, about 65 million years ago. It comprises the Tertiary and Quaternary PERIODS. The Tertiary includes the

Palaeocene, Eocene, Oligocene, Miocene and Pliocene EPOCHS. The Quaternary is made up of the Pleistocene and Holocene (or Recent) epochs. The Holocene opened around 10,000 years ago and is the epoch in which we live.
Calcite, see ARAGONITE.
Cast, or mould, is the impression left in a rock by the inner or outer surface of a fossil. If the cast is of an outer part, a replica of the original organism can be made by pouring into it a rubber solution or plaster of Paris. Sometimes the organ-

The next stages in the sequence are only guessed at. First the pre-biotic material became more concentrated and then it was assembled into protein and nucleic acids. We know that in solutions containing water and the substances we think were present in the Earth's early oceans, droplets will form. These are rich in some of the dissolved substances, and also have an enveloping surface membrane. Such droplets, or COACERVATES, grow as they absorb more of the dissolved substances from the surrounding solution, and may then divide into smaller droplets. Perhaps something of this kind eventually evolved into the earliest cell. In any event, the concentration most likely took place beneath the surface of the oceans, for although ultraviolet light can help simple organic molecules to form, it tends to break down more complex types.

The basic organic molecules are helped to assemble in living organisms by substances called ENZYMES, which form only in the presence of nucleic acids. So in trying to explain how the first nucleic acids developed we seem to be faced with a chicken and egg cycle: enzymes cannot be formed without nucleic acids, and vice-versa. It is possible that metals such as copper, iron or vanadium may have acted instead of enzymes in the chemical reactions that led to the earliest organisms.

These ideas remain only suggestions, and we are still a long way from being able to create life in a test-tube. As we have already seen, even the idea of life evolving spontaneously in a soup of organic molecules is not universally accepted. It has been criticized on several counts, including the lack of direct proof that a soup ever existed. There is, too, the view that the origin of life was extra-terrestrial. In recent years significant amounts of organic molecules have been detected in the space between the stars and in METEORITES. From these and other observations, people have claimed that the first organisms actually developed within COMETS, which 'showered' the Earth with life. If this is true, life-bearing comets could also have seeded other planets, and life might be scattered throughout the universe.

Pre-Cambrian life

It was not until the 1950s that fossil life was confirmed in rocks older than those of the Cambrian geological period, which began about

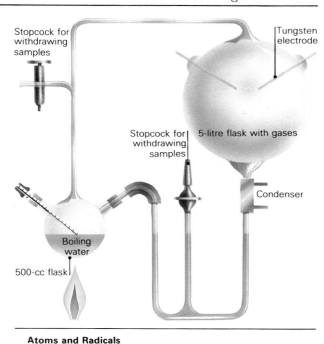

Right: Stanley L. Miller and Harold C. Urey used this equipment at the University of Chicago to simulate electrical discharges in the atmosphere of the primitive Earth. A mixture of gases thought to have been present in the atmosphere at that time were subjected to a spark discharge. The compounds that were then formed were collected in the water at the bottom of the apparatus. Water is boiled and steam is led through the system in order to circulate the gases. The heated gases in the flask are condensed and are then drawn off at intervals in order to be analysed. Electrodes inserted into the flask cause an electric current to be passed through it. The resulting spark provides energy, enabling the gases to react.

Right: Miller and Urey's spark discharge experiments started with simple products that were assumed to have been plentiful in the Earth's early atmosphere. Hydrogen cyanide and aldehydes were given off after a period of spark discharge. Continued sparking produced more complex molecules, including 4 amino acids that are commonly present in proteins — glycine, alanine, aspartic acid and glutamic acid.

Atoms and Radicals

Carbon
Oxygen
Nitrogen
Hydrogen
Radical

Molecules

Hydrogen
Methane
Carbon monoxide
Carbon dioxide
Ammonia
Nitrogen
Water
Hydrogen cyanide
Aldehydes
Glycine
Alanine
Aspartic acid
Glutamic acid

---

ism's remains may have been filled with sediment before they were destroyed and this provides an internal mould. Casts of shells are very common, since the calcium carbonate from which they are made is easily dissolved away from porous rock which allows water to pass through.

Coacervates are small, round particles of organic material (see ORGANIC MOLECULES) dispersed in water. But they are not actually dissolved as in true solutions. Soap and detergents, for example, disperse

in water the same way. It is known that many living substances can dissolve in coacervates or become attached to their surfaces. They could thus have provided important gathering sites for PRE-BIOTIC substances in the earliest oceans.

Comets travel round the Sun, but unlike the planets their orbits are elliptical. They come from a 'cloud' of cometary bodies surrounding the solar system and from time to time individual bodies plunge into it. They are made up of gas, dust and ice, and as they pass the

Sun, its heat causes material to spray out and form a tail which can be seen in the night sky.

D **Darwin,** Charles (1809–82) was a British biologist. Following a voyage to South America and Australasia in HMS *Beagle* in 1831, he developed a theory of evolution (*see page 12*) based on natural selection and survival of the fittest. Only those organisms best fitted to survive, he reasoned, would reproduce and so pass on their characteristics to the

next generation. The balance of characteristics in the

Charles Darwin

descendants might then differ greatly from that in the original. Therefore the organisms would change, or evolve, with the passage of time.

E **Element,** see ATOM.
Enzymes are special kinds of PROTEIN which act as catalysts for chemical reactions inside cells. That is, they speed up the reactions without being changed themselves. Each enzyme performs a specific task in the cell. The fact that the same enzyme may carry out the same task in a wide

570 million years ago. Today we have ample evidence that the varied and complex creatures living in the Cambrian world were preceded by much more primitive ancestors. Their remains show that these were mostly microscopic and single-celled.

The earliest micro-fossils found are simple round cells of the PROKARYOTE type. They are apparently 3,200 million years old and occur in rocks in South Africa. Fossil colonies of prokaryote cells, called STROMATOLITES, also come from slightly younger rocks in Zimbabwe, and are relatively frequent in rocks laid down about 2,300 million years ago. The first traces of more advanced EUKARYOTE cells appear in rocks under 1,500 million years old. Macroscopic remains of multi-celled organisms enter the fossil record only in the last 100 million years of Pre-

Above: Living stromatolite colonies in the Bahamas.

Right: This fossil stromatolite from the Lower Palaeozoic of Europe shows the structure of the algal colony.

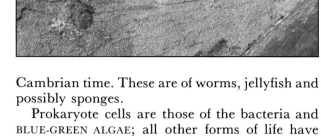

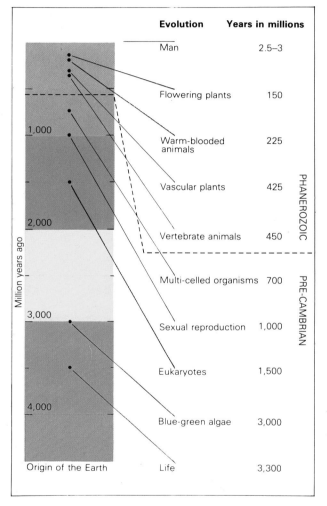

Evolution	Years in millions
Man	2.5–3
Flowering plants	150
Warm-blooded animals	225
Vascular plants	425
Vertebrate animals	450
Multi-celled organisms	700
Sexual reproduction	1,000
Eukaryotes	1,500
Blue-green algae	3,000
Life	3,300

Left: Ten major events in the course of biological evolution are shown, related to the time-scale of the Earth's history. The Phanerozoic, or era of manifest life, began nearly 600 million years ago, for it is in rocks of this age that fossils of organisms with hard parts first appear. The Pre-Cambrian is referred to as the era of hidden life, since the fossil organisms are generally microscopic.

Cambrian time. These are of worms, jellyfish and possibly sponges.

Prokaryote cells are those of the bacteria and BLUE-GREEN ALGAE; all other forms of life have eukaryote cells. The early micro-fossils seem to have been free-floating blue-green algae or their predecessors, while stromatolites were constructed by shallow-water communities of blue-green algae and bacteria. These ancient blue-green algae changed the Earth's atmosphere and in so doing affected the later course of evolution. To understand how this happened, we must first examine the way prokaryotes live.

Food and energy
Blue-green algae make their own foods and so are called AUTOTROPHS. They use sunlight to combine carbon and hydrogen into carbohydrates and release oxygen as waste. Oxygen is then employed to break down the carbohydrates in order to free energy for the organisms. The first process is called photosynthesis; the second respiration. Since both processes occur in the presence of oxygen, they are said to be AEROBIC. Some bacteria are also autotrophs, but they have different pigments for trapping sunlight and the processes are ANAEROBIC, that is, they take place without oxygen. Most bacteria, however, do not make their own food and so are called HETEROTROPHS. They gain their energy by breaking down substances already available. Again this is usually done anaerobically. As well as energy,

range of organisms suggests an evolutionary link between them.
Epochs are sub-divisions of the Tertiary and Quaternary PERIODS and are separated on the basis of fossil types.
Eras are the largest subdivisions of recorded time. The PALAEOZOIC and MESOZOIC eras opened with the appearance of major new groups of organisms, and both closed with the mass extinctions of many descendants of these new groups. The start of the present CAINOZOIC era also coincided with sudden advances in the

evolution of birds and mammals.
Eukaryotes are organisms that have cells with a NUCLEUS (see page 15). In each cell this is surrounded by CYTOPLASM (see page 13) which is relatively large and complex, with several distinct sub-divisions. All green plants, animals and fungi are eukaryotes.

F Fossilization is the process by which remains of organisms, or some trace of their activities, are preserved in rocks and thus form fossils.

G Green algae are EUKARYOTES which have CHLOROPLASTS (see page 17). They range from microscopic single-celled types to large branched seaweeds.

H Heterocysts are thick-walled cells found in BLUE-GREEN ALGAE. They protect nitrogen-fixing ENZYMES from coming into contact with oxygen which would slow them down or stop them altogether.
Heterotrophs are organisms which cannot make the food substances they need from simple non-living

Sea-thong, green algae

materials. Instead they depend directly or indirectly on AUTOTROPHS, mainly plants. Heterotrophs gain their energy by breaking down large, complex molecules such as starch and glucose (see ATOM) derived from autotrophs.

I Isotopes of the same element have the same number of protons (positively charged particles), but a different number of neutrons (particles neither positively nor negatively charged) in their ATOMS. For instance, there are 3

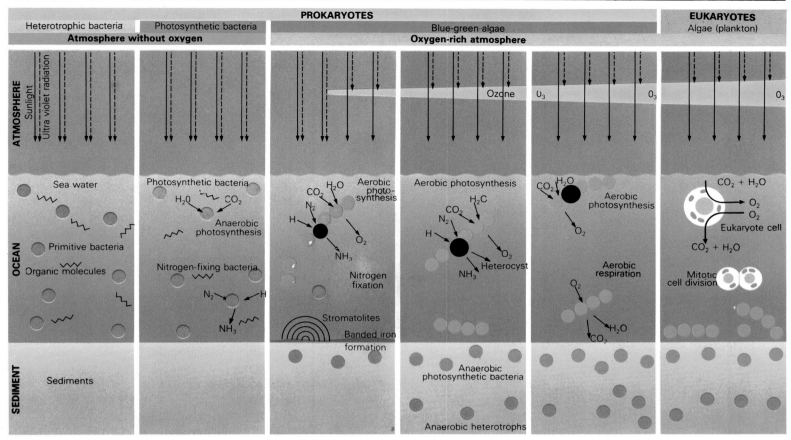

PROKARYOTES					EUKARYOTES
Heterotrophic bacteria	Photosynthetic bacteria		Blue-green algae		Algae (plankton)
Atmosphere without oxygen			**Oxygen-rich atmosphere**		

organisms need nitrogen, to build protein. Only certain prokaryotes can 'fix' nitrogen into a form which can be used by living matter. The enzymes which bring about this fixation will not function if exposed to oxygen, so many nitrogen-fixing bacteria are adapted to oxygen-free environments. Similarly, among the blue-green algae, the enzymes in question are encased in special cells named HETEROCYSTS, to prevent contact with oxygen.

How life developed

These facts and the new fossil evidence available make it possible to reconstruct the likely development of life and of the Earth's atmosphere during the Pre-Cambrian era. The oldest organisms were almost certainly heterotrophic bacteria. These would have 'fed' on the organic molecules which had dissolved in the primeval oceans after being produced in the atmosphere with the aid of ultraviolet light. Bacteria capable of anaerobic

Above: The chart illustrates the evolution of the earliest cells and the influence of an oxygen-rich atmosphere on later evolution. The first primitive bacteria probably lived by fermenting organic molecules in the Earth's early oceans. Later, bacteria capable of photosynthesis and 'fixing' nitrogen appeared. About 2 billion years ago, oxygen-producing photosynthesis began in ancestors of the blue-green algae. This added oxygen to the Earth's atmosphere, while those bacteria unable to live in oxygen retreated to the sediments of the sea-floor. When the oldest eukaryotes evolved the atmosphere was undoubtedly oxygen-rich and the protective ozone layer in the upper atmosphere was already established.

photosynthesis and 'fixing' nitrogen probably evolved next, and it seems that from these the blue-green algae arose, perhaps as far back as 3,000 million years ago. Because stromatolite colonies of these organisms occur so often in rocks laid down around 2,300 million years ago, we can infer that oxygen in the Earth's atmosphere also reached significant proportions about then. This in turn must have led to the ozone layer emerging in the upper atmosphere (which now shields us from harmful ultraviolet rays). As the oxygen increased, the anaerobic bacteria would have retreated to the sediments on the sea-floor where there was little oxygen.

There are other indicators that oxygen was abundant roughly 2,000 million years ago. Compounds of iron and oxygen were widely deposited on the ocean floors at this time, which implies large oxygen reserves. And recently reported are perhaps the oldest fossil heterocyst cells, about 2,200 million years old.

---

isotopes of oxygen: $^{16}_{8}O$ has 8 protons and 8 neutrons; $^{17}_{8}O$ has 8 protons and 9 neutrons; $^{18}_{8}O$ has 8 protons and 10 neutrons. O is the symbol for oxygen; the bottom number given before the symbol states the number of protons, and the top number — the atomic number — gives the sum of protons and neutrons.

K **Kelvin,** William Thomson, Baron (1824–1907) was a British physicist who claimed in 1883 that the surface of the Earth had solidified as recently as 20 to

William Thomson Kelvin, Baron

40 million years ago. This idea was strongly resisted at the time. Scientists believed it was impossible to fit into such a short time span the historical record of rocks and the evolutionary story of life they contained. Though they could not fault Kelvin's calculations, we now realize that these had been based on incomplete information.

L **Lyell,** Sir Charles (1797–1875) was one of the fathers of modern geology (the study of the Earth and its rocks). His book *The Principles of Geology* cham-

pioned the views of James Hutton (1726–97) who developed the theory of uniformitarianism. This states that the processes which took place in rocks during the past were of the same kind as those which operate today. Although this view was highly controversial at first, the uniformitarian approach is central to much research today.

M **Mesozoic** is the name given to an ERA of recorded time. It has 3 PERIODS — the Triassic, Jurassic and Cretaceous. The Mesozoic

extended from 225 to 65 million years ago and is often called the 'Age of Reptiles'. But Mesozoic actually means 'middle life', for it comes between the PALAEOZIC and the CAINOZOIC eras. All 3 coincide with that part of Earth history which is known as the Phanerozoic. This is the time of manifest life, coming after the Pre-Cambrian which until recently was regarded as the time of hidden life.

Meteorites are solid bodies which enter the Earth's atmosphere from space, and may be related to COMETS.

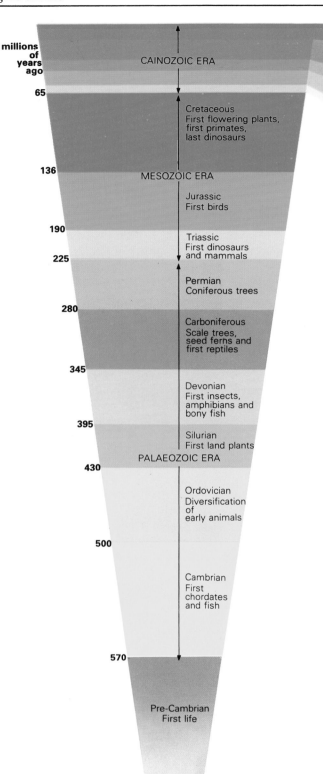

millions of years ago

CAINOZOIC ERA

65

Cretaceous
First flowering plants,
first primates,
last dinosaurs

136

MESOZOIC ERA

Jurassic
First birds

190

Triassic
First dinosaurs
and mammals

225

Permian
Coniferous trees

280

Carboniferous
Scale trees,
seed ferns and
first reptiles

345

Devonian
First insects,
amphibians and
bony fish

395

Silurian
First land plants

PALAEOZOIC ERA

430

Ordovician
Diversification
of
early animals

500

Cambrian
First
chordates
and fish

570

Pre-Cambrian
First life

		millions of years ago
Quaternary	Recent or Holocene	
	Pleistocene	1.6
	Pliocene	7
Tertiary	Miocene	
		26
	Oligocene	37.5
	Eocene	53
	Palaeocene	65

Left: Geological time is divided into eras, which are in turn divided into periods. The Tertiary and Quaternary periods are further sub-divided into epochs. The various divisions coincide with the appearance and disappearance of different groups of fossil organisms.

Everything points to the atmosphere having been oxygen-rich when the first eukaryote cells appeared, less than 1,500 million years ago. They resembled GREEN ALGAE and probably respired aerobically, as did all later eukaryotes.

The Earth's history

Rocks and fossil remains of plants or animals preserved in them provide a record of the Earth's history. They show that life has grown more varied and complex, and that great changes in climate have taken place, as has the distribution of land and sea. Where STRATA (or layers of rock) rest upon each other, the highest will be the youngest, provided the strata have not been overturned by earth movements. Therefore a study moving upwards through the strata and the fossils they contain will reveal successively younger stages of the Earth's history. Studies of this kind have led to a way of classifying rocks according to their relative — rather than their actual — ages.

The time which has elapsed since the Pre-Cambrian ERA is divided into three more eras: the PALAEOZOIC, the MESOZOIC and the CAINOZOIC. The rocks of each of these three eras are further divided into SYSTEMS which correspond to the different PERIODS of geological time. The two Cainozoic periods — the Tertiary and the Quaternary — are broken down again into EPOCHS. There are just two in the Quaternary: the Pleistocene and the Holocene. The Holocene is the epoch in which we live.

Dating of rocks

Before the relatively recent arrival of accurate geological dating, various early estimates were made of the actual ages of the Earth and its rocks. Charles LYELL worked from supposed rates of change in the fossil populations of one group of animals — the molluscs. From this he obtained

---

They are made up of iron or stone, or a mixture of both. Most meteorites are stony, and one group (the so-called carbonaceous chondrites) contains ORGANIC MOLECULES.

Piece of a meteorite

Mid-oceanic ridges are long narrow mountain chains which rise from the sea-floor. They mark the meeting point of the great rigid slabs which support the continents and oceans. Molten rock from the Earth's centre wells up at the ridges and, when cooled, adds new crust to the edges of the rigid plates, as they constantly spread apart from each other.
Molecules, see ATOM.

N **Nucleic acids** are made up from a ribose sugar, a phosphate group

and a few relatively simple nitrogen substances called bases.

O **Organic molecules** contain ATOMS of carbon and hydrogen. The organic molecules essential to life also contain atoms from one or more other elements, especially nitrogen, oxygen, phosphorus and sulphur.
Ozone is a gas in which each molecule comprises 3 atoms of oxygen (hence its chemical formula O_3). Ozone is concentrated into a layer in the upper atmosphere. Unlike other components in

the atmosphere it absorbs ULTRAVIOLET LIGHT, so that only small amounts manage to penetrate as far as the Earth's surface.

P **Palaeomagnetism** refers to the fossil magnetization of rocks. As rocks containing iron minerals are laid down, or as molten rocks cool, they take on a weak magnetization which runs parallel to the Earth's magnetic field. The pattern of the field resembles that which a giant bar magnet would produce if placed parallel to the Earth's axis.

Palaeozoic means 'ancient life' and is the name given to an ERA of recorded time which lasted from 570 to 225 million years ago. The Palaeozoic spans 6 PERIODS – the Cambrian, Ordovician, Silurian, Devonian, Carboniferous and Permian.
Panspermia was a theory developed by ARRHENIUS. It stated that life arrived on Earth in the form of a bacterial spore which had escaped from a distant planet. In its original form the theory has been rejected, since in space the spore would have been subjected

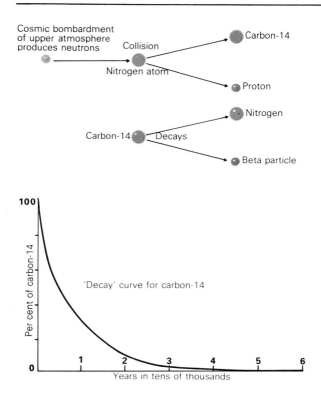

'Decay' curve for carbon-14

Per cent of carbon-14

Years in tens of thousands

Left: This diagram shows the development of carbon-14 in the upper atmosphere. Carbon-14 can be used to date once-living materials. Cosmic bombardment of the upper atmosphere produces neutrons. These collide with atoms of nitrogen to produce carbon-14 and protons. Carbon-14 is taken up by living organisms, but after their death it decays at a constant rate into nitrogen and beta particles. The amount of carbon-14 in their remains is halved every 5,570 years. After about 55,000 years there is very little left, and so the carbon-14 dating method cannot be used for remains older than this.

which are considered to be the same age as the Earth, and of 3,400 million years for the oldest known Earth rocks. Rocks as young as 30,000 years old can also be dated by the potassium-argon method. But dates as far back as 50,000 years are gained from measuring amounts of a radioactive isotope of carbon found in the remains of organisms. The relative amounts of the isotope and of stable carbon present in the organisms while they were alive can be judged fairly accurately. So the quantity of the isotope in their remains gives a measure of their age. Practically all of the isotope decays into nitrogen in 55,000 years, which explains the limited range of carbon dating.

Radioactive dating has been applied to the studies of PALAEOMAGNETISM and SEA-FLOOR SPREADING. Alternate periods of normal and reversed magnetism in the Earth's magnetic field are recorded in cores of sediments from the sea bed. They are also recorded as parallel strips in the lavas which cover the floor of the oceans either side of the MID-OCEANIC RIDGES. These strips formed from lavas that welled up and cooled at the ridges, and were then carried away

ages of 80 million years for the start of the Tertiary period, and 240 million years for the start of the Cambrian. Another early calculation was based on the rates at which it was thought certain kinds of rocks were laid down. This put the opening of the Cambrian at about 600 million years ago. We now know that the first and the third of these estimates were surprisingly good. Yet later, in 1883, William KELVIN worked out that the Earth was no more than 40 million years old, assuming that it had cooled from an original molten state. He was mistaken partly because he did not know that the Earth contains unstable radioactive elements (see RADIOACTIVITY). As these decay they release heat and so slow down the rate at which the Earth cools.

Measurement of radioactive elements and their decay products is today the standard way to date rocks. The most useful measurement is that of an ISOTOPE of potassium as it decays into an isotope of argon. As we know the rate at which this change takes place, we can measure how much of each isotope exists in a rock and work out its age. Potassium-argon dates of 4,600 million years have been obtained for meteorites,

Right: A study of the ocean floor has revealed that on either side of the mid-oceanic ridges, iron minerals in its rocks are lined up with the Earth's magnetic field. Strips of reversed and normal magnetization form the same pattern on either side of the ridges (*top*), as the Earth's magnetic field has alternated between normal and reversed. Matching alternations are also recorded in sediments which have accumulated on the ocean floor (*below*). The epochs of normal and reversed magnetization, and the shorter reversals or events within them, have been dated by the potassium-argon method. Measuring the magnetic polarity of sea-floor sediments therefore provides a ready magnetic chronology or timescale.

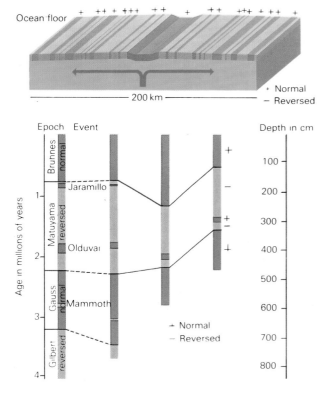

Ocean floor

200 km

+ Normal
− Reversed

Epoch   Event

Brunnes — normal
Matuyama — reversed
Gauss — normal
Gilbert — reversed

Jaramillo
Olduvai
Mammoth

Age in millions of years

Depth in cm

+ Normal
− Reversed

to amounts of radiation several times above that needed to kill any Earth-living spore. That a spore or cell arrived on Earth in a meteorite, however, is not so readily disproved.

Pasteur, Louis (1822–95) was a French scientist who, among other great achievements, designed experiments which finally proved wrong the theory of spontaneous generation (*see page 3*). He established that certain organic substances (*see* ORGANIC MOLECULES) are broken down by micro-organisms in the atmos-

phere, and that this decomposition cannot happen in their absence.

Periods are sub-divisions of ERAS and each is identified with specific fossil plants and animals.

Permafrost is the permanently frozen ground of arctic and antarctic regions, such as the tundra beyond the northern coniferous forests. During the glacial stages of the Pleistocene, permafrost was extensive in the mid-northern hemisphere. The soils in these regions often display features of former permafrost.

Permafrost in Siberia

Photosynthesis is a process by which living organisms make sugar out of water and carbon dioxide. The energy for this synthesis is provided by sunlight, which is captured by a green pigment known as chlorophyll. ENZYMES convert some of the sugar into starch for storage, and the rest is broken down to free energy during respiration (*see page 6*). In EUKARYOTES chlorophyll is concentrated in structures called chloroplasts, and some people have suggested that these are the descendants of former free-

living microscopic organisms.

Pre-biotic means 'before life'. The term is often used of chemical substances which we assume formed in the atmosphere and oceans of the early Earth and from which the first living organisms are believed to have developed. Some scientists have pointed out, however, that there is no direct evidence for these pre-biotic substances being manufactured on Earth, although they do appear to be plentiful in inter-stellar space. These scientists therefore

sideways as the ocean floors expanded. As they cooled, the lavas were imprinted by the Earth's magnetic field. Potassium-argon dates for the normal and reversed periods show that the ocean floors have spread from the ridges at between 10–100 millimetres each year.

How a fossil is formed

In order for organisms or traces of their activities to appear in the fossil record they must be preserved. Many organisms are eaten by predators. The dead remains of those left will normally decompose or be destroyed by scavengers, winds, waves and currents. Even after FOSSILIZATION, the remains of an organism may still be destroyed by chemical action. In other words, fossils are rarely a representative sample of former plant and animal communities.

More distortion is introduced because usually only the hard parts of an organism, such as teeth, bones and shells, are preserved. The fossil may be of the hard part itself, or perhaps a CAST of its inside or outside. Soft parts and entirely soft-bodied organisms are known mostly from impressions left in the sediments which buried them. Very rarely indeed, such impressions may also indicate what colour the organism was. It is clear that when a group of organisms evolved hard parts their chances of being fossilized must have greatly increased. Perhaps this explains why so many new forms of life appear abruptly in the fossil record at the beginning of the Cambrian period.

Preservation is most likely where the dead organism is saved from destruction. On land this happens only in special situations. For example, insects may be entombed in tree resin which later fossilizes into AMBER. Much more common is the preservation in peat bogs of plant materials, bones and, occasionally, soft parts. But most spectacular of all are the frozen mammoths in the PERMAFROST of Siberia.

Marine fossils

Marine environments are much more favourable than the land for fossilization, as large parts of the sea-floor are continuously buried by sediment from rivers. But the remains of marine organisms are often chemically rearranged or altered during the process of fossilization. For example, some modern shells are made from one form of calcium

Right: The process of fossilization takes place in various ways. In the scenes shown here, for example, a mangrove swamp is gradually submerged by water, and, as sea level rises, the remains of its vegetation are eventually buried beneath marine sediments. Animals with shells, particularly gastropods, flourish in the shallow coastal waters. In turn, their remains are covered by sediments carried down by rivers. A further rise in sea level produces a deeper-water environment, in which fish are the dominant types of animal. Their skeletons accumulate in the muds of the sea floor. In time, sea level falls dramatically, and the sea floor becomes land once more. Beneath the new land surface are successive layers of rock which contain fossils of fish, the gastropods, and the trunks of trees which once grew in the mangrove swamp.

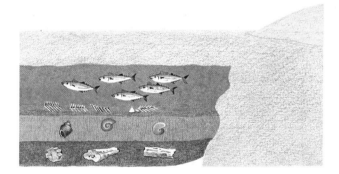

Rock strata, Lulworth Cove, England

Left: A fossil ammonite, *Anahoplites,* from the Gault Clay of south-east England. The outer form of the shell has been preserved in iron pyrites, which tends to disintegrate when exposed to air.

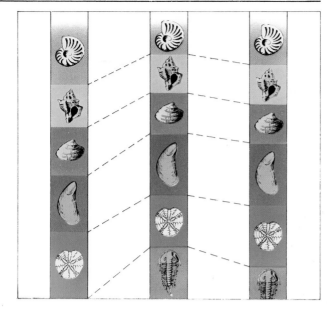

Above: Fossils are used in the relative dating of rocks. The presence of a specific type of ammonite, for example, will often allow the palaeontologist to relate the rock in which it is found to a particular zone or stage of a geological system. Fossils also help to relate strata over considerable distances (as in the matching coloured blocks in the diagram which represent successive strata), even if they look different.

carbonate known as ARAGONITE, which through time often changes into a more stable form called calcite. So although aragonite shells are common in Cainozoic rocks, and to a lesser extent in Mesozoic ones, they are hardly known in older rocks. In other cases, the hard parts are impregnated or replaced by calcite, SILICA or iron compounds from water surrounding the remains. However, the outside form of the fossil is not changed, and in those made of iron pyrites the details are often very sharp. The last kind of change is that where the soft parts lose their more volatile substances and leave a carbon-rich residue, which may trace the outline of the organism.

What fossils tell

Fossils are used to date rocks and reconstruct past environments. For example, there may be two layers of rock, one of which yields a large variety of fossils. The other may contain a much smaller variety, but of organisms known to have lived within a short geological time span. In practice, both layers could be related not only to their geological periods or epochs, but probably also to their respective STAGES and maybe to their ZONES as well. This is one of the ways in which geologists recognize different rock units and follow them across country when making geological maps. Exactly the same principle is used to identify rock layers reached in bore holes.

Below: A petrified tree trunk, in which the original wood has been replaced by silica. This specimen is from Arizona, USA.

of ATOMS of silicon and oxygen. A common form is quartz — a hard, glassy substance. The majority of sand grains on most beaches are composed of quartz.

Stages are sub-divisions of SYSTEMS, and are recognized by their particular groups of fossils. Usually a stage is a succession of ZONES.

Strata is the collective name for layers of rock, an individual layer being a stratum. Strata may vary considerably in both thickness and width.

Stromatolites are reef-like communities of BLUE-GREEN ALGAE and BACTERIA. Living examples have only recently been recognized, as sea creatures feed on them, so preventing their development into significant structures. However, such creatures had not evolved in the Pre-Cambrian era, and large stromatolite colonies were therefore quite common then.

Systems are the sequences of rocks which correspond to individual PERIODS.

U **Ultraviolet light** has a shorter wavelength than that of visible light.

V **Viruses** are generally much smaller than the smallest BACTERIA. They have no NUCLEUS or CYTOPLASM (*see pages 15, 13*), and consist almost entirely of DNA (*see page 13*) or RNA (*see page 15*), usually with a PROTEIN covering. All viruses live as parasites on higher organisms and cannot reproduce without the aid of the ENZYMES of their host. Since they depend on other organisms for their continued survival, some scientists believe that viruses must have evolved after cellular forms of life such as bacteria. On the other hand, their very primitive characteristics have been said to indicate an origin earlier than cells. But, because they are unable to reproduce independently, it has also been argued that

A virus

they should not be seen as living organisms at all. Certainly they seem to occupy a twilight zone between life and non-life.

Z **Zone** refers to the rock stratum or STRATA laid down in a specific interval of time and which can be identified by particular kinds of fossil organisms. Although 2 sets of strata may be very different in composition and thickness, if they have the same zonal fossils they belong to the same zone. The zones take their names from the zonal fossils.

The millions of plants and animals which live on the Earth today have evolved to their present forms throughout the history of our planet. This process involves environmental selection and biological inheritance.

Theories of Evolution

Organisms change with time and such change is called evolution. It was once widely believed that all plants and animals had been specially created in their present form. The first serious challenge to this view was made by Jean LAMARCK in the early 1800s. He thought that organisms had started by spontaneous generation (*see page 3*), but that over time each had become better adapted to its environment through inheriting acquired characteristics from its parents. According to this idea giraffe necks became longer from repeatedly stretching for tree leaves, and the added length achieved in one generation was inherited by the next.

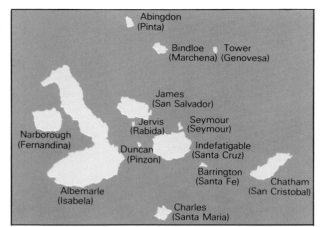

Abingdon

Duncan

Albemarle

Above: Each island in the Galapagos archipelago has its own type of tortoise (*right*). The 2 longer-necked species shown live in dry places and feed on tree cacti, whereas the short-necked species lives in moist regions and feeds off more luxuriant, low-growing vegetation.

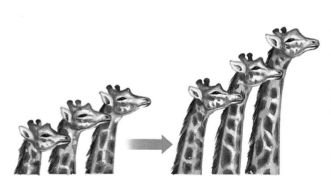

Left: Lamarck believed that giraffe necks had become longer from repeatedly stretching for tree leaves (*top*) and that the long necks achieved in one generation had been inherited by the next. According to Darwin's views, however, selection would favour individuals with the longest necks (*below*). Over the generations the length of the neck would progressively increase, but there would still be room for variations.

In 1844 DARWIN (*see page 5*) presented a different view of ADAPTIVE EVOLUTION. Put simply, all individuals in a plant or animal SPECIES vary in some way, and together they produce more offspring than can survive. The environment in which they live will determine which individuals are best fitted to survive, and only those so 'selected' will therefore reproduce. In the case of the giraffe, selection favoured individuals with the longest necks, so that over the generations the length of the neck progressively increased. Where a population of one species is broken up, say by a rise in sea-level, then the changes resulting from selection in each of the now separate groups could well differ. They might even diverge to the point where individuals from one group could no longer interbreed with those of another. This reasoning

---

Reference

A **Adaptive evolution** results in organisms becoming better fitted to the environments in which they live. The fit is so close that for a long time organisms were thought to have been created in their present form by a supernatural force. However, becoming adapted to an environment is the end product of a series of changes in organisms over time — changes which favoured their chances of

survival through natural selection (*see page 12*). Because there was so much variation between individuals in populations which were the ancestors of living organisms, some were better equipped than others to survive. Only the survivors reproduced, so that it was their characteristics which were passed on to the next generation. The process was repeated over and over again and in this way many organisms have come to differ greatly from their predecessors. For example, speed was essential for the

zebra's forebears to survive, and so down the ages their legs became progressively longer and their toes were reduced to one.
Amino acids are the chemical building blocks of PROTEIN (*see page 10*). Their general formula is R CH (NH$_2$) COOH, where R is a side group of any atoms, usually carbon and hydrogen. When amino acids are linked into chains to form protein, a molecule of water (H$_2$O) is removed at each linkage point. Twenty different amino acids are found in protein, and their number and combination

control specific types of protein. Since amino acids can combine in so many diffe-

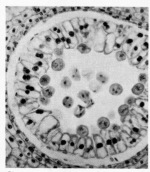
Chromosomes in a cell

rent ways, it is not surprising that thousands of proteins are known.
Asexual reproduction occurs when one or more offspring develop from a parent organism without the aid of GAMETES, or sex cells.

C **Chromosomes** are usually included in the cell NUCLEUS. Each is made up of a central strand of one very long DNA molecule, which in turn comprises hundreds of GENES. Around the DNA molecule there are proteins called histones. Genes which are covered by

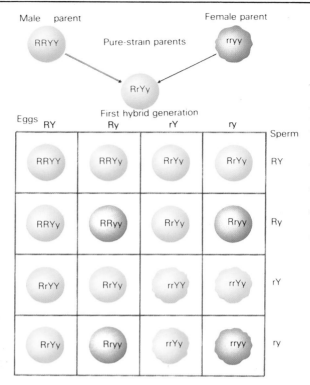

Male parent
RRYY
Pure-strain parents
Female parent
rryy

RrYy
First hybrid generation

Eggs

	RY	Ry	rY	ry	Sperm
	RRYY	RRYy	RrYy	RrYy	RY
	RRYy	RRyy	RrYy	Rryy	Ry
	RrYY	RrYy	rrYY	rrYy	rY
	RrYy	Rryy	rrYy	rryy	ry

Left: If a male pea plant with only dominant genes for round, yellow (RRYY) peas is crossed with a female pea plant with only recessive genes for wrinkled, green (rryy) peas, the offspring have mixed genes, though they will only produce peas with the dominant round, yellow traits. When the first generation plants are crossed, however, the wrinkled and green traits reappear in a constant ratio to the yellow and round ones. There are always 3 times as many yellow ones and 3 times as many round ones.

was used by Darwin to explain the different but closely related species of tortoises and birds on each island in the Galapagos.

How heredity works

However, Darwin could not explain what caused the variation between individuals on which selection depends. This was made clear by Gregor MENDEL in his experiments with peas. He found that the characteristics passed on to each generation are controlled by inherited units, which we now call GENES. He cross-bred pure strains of round, yellow peas with wrinkled, green ones and found that the first generation of offspring were all round and yellow. When these in turn were crossed, four kinds of peas resulted. In every 16, 9 were round and yellow, 3 round and green, 3 wrinkled and yellow and 1 was wrinkled and green. From this he worked out that each of the original peas had two equivalent genes for colour and two equivalent genes for shape. The genes for yellow colour and round shape he described as DOMINANT; those for green colour and wrinkled shape as RECESSIVE. In the first generation of peas only the dominant genes were expressed, making all the offspring round

and yellow. In the second generation the recessive green and wrinkled ones were 're-vealed', but only where they were responsible for colour or shape.

Genes make up strands called CHROMOSOMES, which in all EUKARYOTES (*see page 6*) are in the cell NUCLEUS. Just as there are pairs of equivalent genes, so in most cells there are matching sets (2N) of the basic number of chromosomes (N). In ASEXUAL reproduction the number of chromosomes doubles (to 4N) before the parent cell divides. Each daughter cell then has the correct amount (2N) of chromosomes. This process is known as MITOSIS. In SEXUAL reproduction the cell division is called MEIOSIS. Here the same chromosome doubling (to 4N) takes place, but the chromosomes segregate in a different way prior to cell division. The new cells therefore have the same number of chromosomes (2N) as the parent cell, but in different combinations. A second division then follows to produce sex cells, or GAMETES, which have 50 per cent (N) of the normal number of chromosomes (2N). When two gametes (usually a male and female) unite they

Below: Meiosis (the process of cell division in sexual reproduction) taking place in an organism with matching sets (2N) of the basic number of chromosomes (N). The result is a set of cells which has only 50% of the chromosomes of the parent cell. The parent cell may initially divide in 1 of 2 ways, so far as the combination of chromosomes is concerned. In practice, therefore, 2 different sets of sex cells, or gametes, are possible. As the cell divides, portions of matching chromosomes often stick together and genetic material is exchanged between the chromosomes. This 'crossing-over' is a further source of genetic variation.

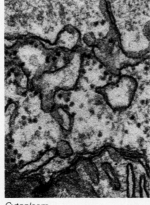

2N = 4

4N

Either — Nuclear division — Or

First meiotic division

2N   2N   Second meiotic division   2N   2N

N   N   N   N   N   N   N   N

---

histones cannot control the making of protein and vice versa. Chromosomes occur in pairs in most cells. Both members of a pair are identical in appearance and are called homologous chromosomes. The number of paired chromosomes in a cell varies from SPECIES to species. Man, for example, has 23 pairs.

Codons are non-overlapping triplets of NUC-LEOTIDE bases. Each codon corresponds to an AMINO ACID. The 4 different nucleotide bases can combine into 64 possible triplets. But the 64

triplet sequences corres-pond to only 20 amino acids and such instructions as 'start' and 'stop'. It is there-fore clear that some amino acids are dictated by more than one codon.

Cytoplasm is the material found inside the cell membrane or cell wall. It also occurs outside the NUCLEUS or (if the cell has no nucleus) the loop of DNA.

D **DNA** is short for deoxy-ribonucleic acid. DNA occurs as giant molecules and in most organisms is the store of genetic information

Cytoplasm

(*see* GENE) which is dupli-cated and passed on to the NUCLEUS of daughter cells. DNA molecules are made up of 4 different types of NUC-LEOTIDES.

Dominant characteristics are those which tend to prevail in each new genera-tion of organisms. In humans, one pair of CHROMO-SOMES carries GENES for eye colour. If one parent has eye colour genes which are both brown and the other's genes are both for blue, they will always have brown-eyed children. So in this case the gene for brown eye colour is

dominant over that for blue eyes.

G **Gametes** are reproduc-tive, or sex, cells. During sexual reproduction 2 ga-metes unite to form a ZYGOTE.

Genes are chemical codes which control the making of proteins — the structural matter of life. Each gene carries the information needed to produce one pro-tein. A gene has more than one state, and so in practice gives rise to slightly different proteins. These different states cause variations in the same SPECIES.

form a ZYGOTE with the normal number (2N) of chromosomes, and the zygote then develops into a new organism. Sexual re-shuffling of the genes into new combinations through meiosis produced the contrasts that Mendel observed in his peas.

The genetic code

The gene strands, or chromosomes, are actually very long DNA molecules. Each molecule is shaped rather like a spiral staircase. The 'sides' are made up of two identical chains of alternate sugar and phosphate molecules. The 'steps' joining these chains each have a pair of substances called bases, of which there are four: adenine, thymine, guanine and cytosine — A, T, G and C for short. A always joins with T to form a step, and G with C. The staircase is built up first of all from units called NUCLEOTIDES. Every nucleotide has a sugar molecule and a phosphate molecule — in effect a section of one staircase side—to which one of the four bases is attached. The way in which nucleotides are arranged into DNA is therefore decided by the way in which the bases are paired. And the possible combinations of paired bases are endless. When a chromosome doubles, the DNA molecule 'unzips' itself. Unpaired bases then link up with nucleotides in the cell nucleus to form two new molecules of DNA. In this way genetic information in the chromosome is passed on, by the gametes, down through the generations.

Mendel's hereditary units correspond to segments of the DNA molecule which are identified as triplets of bases, for example: AGT, TCA, GCA or CGT. A triplet is a sort of 'code word'

for making one of the AMINO ACIDS which are the sole ingredients of protein. A specific sequence of triplets is therefore a code for a certain kind of protein. Such a sequence makes one hereditary unit (or one gene). Although a multitude of proteins exists in living organisms, they are all assembled from just 20 common amino acids.

How proteins form

Protein is formed in the CYTOPLASM surrounding the cell nucleus, by a substance called RNA, a near-relative of DNA. Spirally-coiled nucleotide chains in the DNA molecule separate slightly to form a PUFF, which then travels along the molecule. While the chains are apart, nucleotides

Below: The gene strands, or chromosomes, contain all the genetic information carried in the body's cells. Every chromosome is made up of 2 chromatids, each of which is an immensely long, coiled molecule of DNA. The DNA molecule itself is rather like a spiral staircase, with sides made up of sugar and phosphate molecules. Joining these are cross-pieces, or 'steps', each of which has a pair of 4 bases— adenine, guanine, thymine and cytosine. These bases, or chemical units, can appear in an infinitely variable order, and the order of the paired links makes up the coded instructions which can be used elsewhere in the cell. When the cell is ready to divide, the DNA must be replicated exactly, so that each new cell will have the same type of DNA. This happens when the DNA splits. The chemical units which form the cross-links snap on to the ends of the split cross-links, forming 2 identical new strands of DNA.

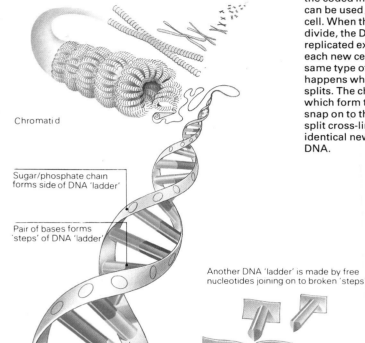

Chromatid

Sugar/phosphate chain forms side of DNA 'ladder'

Pair of bases forms 'steps' of DNA 'ladder'

Another DNA 'ladder' is made by free nucleotides joining on to broken 'steps'

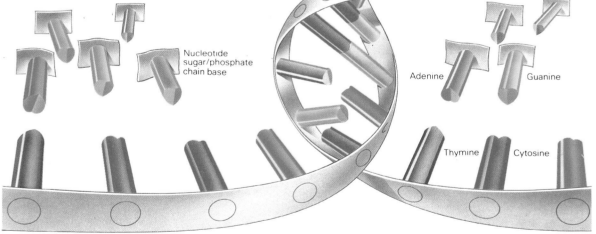

Nucleotide sugar/phosphate chain base

Adenine   Guanine

Thymine   Cytosine

L Lamarck, Jean-Baptiste (1744–1829), was a French biologist whose theory of evolution rightly recognized that organisms had become better adapted to their environments over time, and that the diversity of life was due to adaptation. But his theory was faulty as it assumed that characteristics acquired during an organism's lifetime are passed on to its offspring. Although the inheriting of acquired characteristics has not been completely disproved, it is obvious that many (such as the loss of a limb in an

Jean-Baptiste Lamarck

accident, for example) are not inherited by the next generation.

M Meiosis is the process of cell division which takes place at some stage in the life of all organisms with SEXUAL REPRODUCTION. It results in 4 daughter cells with nuclei containing half the number of CHROMOSOMES of the parental NUCLEUS.
Mendel, Gregor (1822–84), was an Austrian monk who founded the scientific study of heredity or genetics. From experiments in which he crossed different kinds of

Gregor Mendel

pea plants, he established that heredity characteristics are passed on by units which we now call GENES.
Mitosis is the process of cell division which produces new cells or individuals with CHROMOSOMES identical to those of the parent.
Mutations are errors in duplicating DNA which may lead to the production of different proteins. Mutations may be restricted to GENES or may affect larger parts of the CHROMOSOME. If mutations occur in an organism's sex cells they can be passed on to the next generation.

line up against one of them, in a sequence decided by the positions of the bases, to form RNA. (The bases in RNA are the same as in DNA, except that thymine is replaced by the closely related uracil, or U.) As the chains connect once more, RNA is released as a strand of nucleotides with unpaired bases. It enters the cytoplasm where it acts as template, or copy, for the making of protein.

This 'messenger' RNA attaches itself to a RIBOSOME, which moves along the nucleotide strand 'reading' the coded message. At the same time molecules of another kind of RNA, transfer RNA, carry to the ribosome the amino acids that match their triplets of bases. The ribosome then assembles the amino acids into a protein chain, according to the instructions coded on the messenger RNA.

All organisms have the same set of RNA CODONS. Since there are four bases which can combine into different groups of three, there are altogether 64 triplet codons. Not only do they

First RNA nucleotide base	Second RNA nucleotide base				Third RNA nucleotide base
	U	C	A	G	
Uracil (U)	Phenylaniline	Serine	Tyrosine	Cysteine	U
	Phenylaniline	Serine	Tyrosine	Cysteine	C
	Leucine	Serine	STOP	STOP	A
	Leucine	Serine	STOP	Tryptophan	G
Cytosine (C)	Leucine	Proline	Histidine	Arginine	U
	Leucine	Proline	Histidine	Arginine	C
	Leucine	Proline	Glutamine	Arginine	A
	Leucine	Proline	Glutamine	Arginine	G
Adenine (A)	Isoleucine	Threonine	Asparagine	Serine	U
	Isoleucine	Threonine	Asparagine	Serine	C
	Isoleucine	Threonine	Lysine	Arginine	A
	START/Methionine	Threonine	Lysine	Arginine	G
Guanine (G)	Valine	Alanine	Aspartic acid	Glycine	U
	Valine	Alanine	Aspartic acid	Glycine	C
	Valine	Alanine	Glutamic acid	Glycine	A
	Valine	Alanine	Glutamic acid	Glycine	G

Neutral   Aromatic   Basic   Acidic   Sulphur containing

Above: Triplets of nucleotide bases act as signals for the manufacture of 20 amino acids. They also specify 'start' and 'stop', to signal the beginning and end of the assembly of amino acids that correspond to a specific protein. For example, Uracil (first base) with Adenine (A — second base) plus Adenine (A — third base) equal 'stop'. Since only 20 amino acids are specified by 64 signals, the genetic code is highly redundant (e.g. UAA, UAG and UGA all specify 'stop').

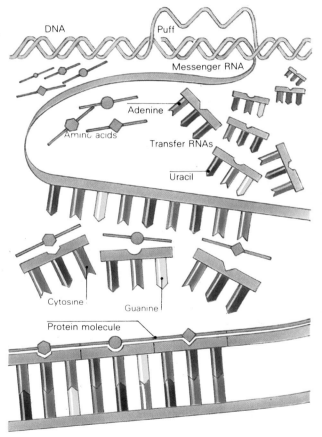

Left: How the information in the DNA molecule is used to make protein. Messenger RNA copies the genetic code from DNA when the DNA coils separate to form a puff. It then carries its copy of the code to the ribosome. As the ribosome moves along the RNA strand 'reading' the coded message, transfer RNAs convey to the ribosome the amino acids that match their triplets of bases. Here they are assembled into protein in a sequence dictated by the messenger RNA.

(figure labels: DNA, Puff, Messenger RNA, Adenine, Amino acids, Transfer RNAs, Uracil, Cytosine, Guanine, Protein molecule)

inform the ribosome of the order in which to assemble the amino acids, they also instruct it where to start and stop. Thus AUG serves as a 'start' signal, whereas UAA, UAG and UGA signify 'stop'. As three triplets can specify 'stop', it appears that the genetic code involves some redundancy. For instance, out of the 20 acids specified by the 64 codons, eight are each specified by four or more different triplets.

Mistakes in the code

Any error in producing a replica of the DNA molecule during meiosis could affect protein assembly in the developing offspring. Such errors produce MUTATIONS. In point mutations one pair of nucleotide bases replaces another. Because of the redundancy in the genetic code this need have no practical effect. But it could lead to one amino acid being substituted for another, or even to the triplet of bases being altered so as to specify the 'stop' signal. Larger mutations arise when a nucleotide is put in or taken out. Small mutations are the basic source of most variety in a population, as they spread in ever-different combinations by sexual reproduction. Natural selection eventually decides if a small mutation is of advantage to organisms. Large mutations tend not to be so.

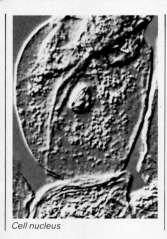

Cell nucleus

N **Nucleotides** are combinations of phosphate, sugar and 1 of 4 bases — adenine, thymine, guanine and cytosine.
Nucleus is the membrane-bound body which contains the CHROMOSOMES in a EUKARYOTE (*see page 6*) cell.

P **Puff** is that part of the DNA molecule which uncoils slightly to allow access to the information recorded in the GENE sequence of a single DNA strand. This sequence is used as a pattern to be copied for making messenger RNA.

R **Recessive** characteristics are those which are least likely to prevail in each new generation. A recessive character appears only when both GENES for that characteristic are recessive. Where a DOMINANT and a recessive gene for a characteristic occur in the same organism, it is always the dominant gene which is expressed, or revealed.
Ribosomes are the sites at which protein synthesis takes place in a cell.
RNA stands for ribonucleic acid. Messenger RNA copies the genetic code from DNA

and carries it to the RIBOSOME, where it dictates the sequence in which AMINO ACIDS are assembled into proteins. Transfer RNA carries the amino acids to the ribosome.

S **Sexual reproduction** involves the fusion of male and female sex cells or GAMETES.
Species are groups of organisms which are distinct from other groups by their GENES. Members of one species can breed with each other, but not with members of other species.

Z **Zygote** is a cell formed by the union of 2 GAMETES.

A formed zygote

16

Evolution of Plants

From their primitive beginnings in water, plants have adapted to a way of life away from it, in all the diverse habitats of land.

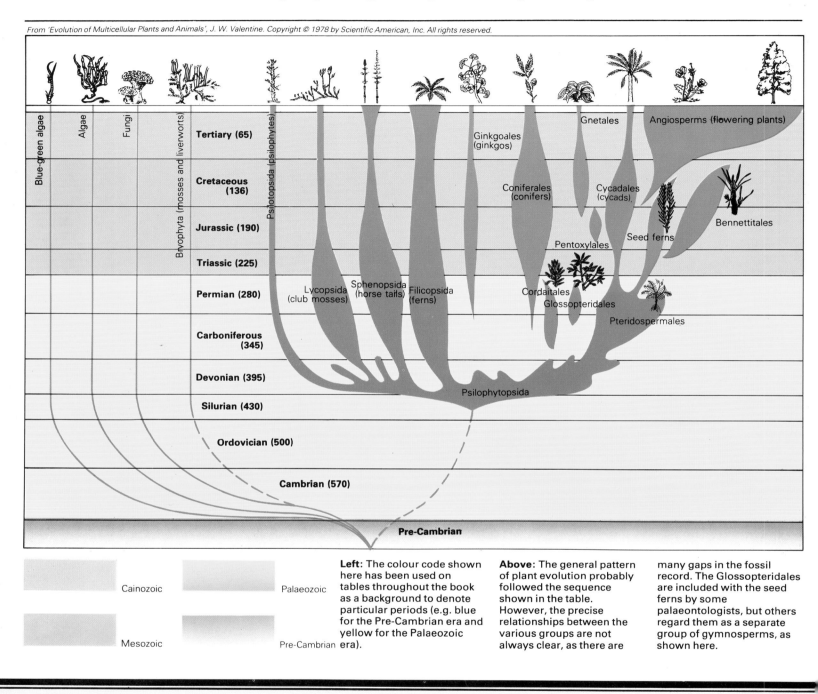

Left: The colour code shown here has been used on tables throughout the book as a background to denote particular periods (e.g. blue for the Pre-Cambrian era and yellow for the Palaeozoic era).

Cainozoic

Mesozoic

Palaeozoic

Pre-Cambrian

Above: The general pattern of plant evolution probably followed the sequence shown in the table. However, the precise relationships between the various groups are not always clear, as there are many gaps in the fossil record. The Glossopteridales are included with the seed ferns by some palaeontologists, but others regard them as a separate group of gymnosperms, as shown here.

Reference

A Angiospermae are a sub-division of the seed plants, or SPERMATOPHYTA. The angiosperms are the highest form of seed plants. They are also known as the flowering plants, and their seeds are always enclosed in fruits.

Annularia are leaf fossils of CALAMITES in which the leaves are arranged in whorls. Unlike those in ASTEROPHYL-LITES, however, the leaves tend to stand out at right angles from the stem and are shaped like elongated ovals.

Asterophyllites are leaf fossils of CALAMITES in which the leaves are arranged in whorls. Each whorl has needle-like leaves, which tend to be cupped upwards.

B Bennettitales are an extinct order of the GYM-NOSPERMAE. They were palm-like plants with reproductive organs that strongly resembled the flower of ANGIOSPER-MAE. They lived from the Triassic up until Cretaceous times.

Bryophyta are a division of the plant kingdom which includes the mosses and liverworts. They lack VASCU-LAR TISSUES but possess an-choring RHIZOIDS. These plants have 2 alternate gen-erations — GAMETOPHYTE and SPOROPHYTE. Unlike PTERIDOPHYTA, in bryophytes the gametophyte generation is the adult plant. It is neces-sary for this to live in moist places since the male sex cells it produces need to make use of a film of water in order to swim to the female sex organs, which are on the same adult plant.

C Calamites are fossil CASTS *(see page 4)* of the inner stems of plants be-longing to the SPHENOPSIDA. They thrived in the Car-boniferous and many looked like a giant version of EQUISETUM.

Carpels are the female structures found in the centre of most flowers. A single carpel consists of an OVARY which contains one or more OVULES which in turn contain the sex cells. The top of the ovary is drawn up into

Calamites

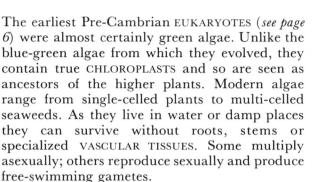

Left: Internal mould of a *Calamites* stem, from the Carboniferous coal swamps. This specimen was found at Snowden Colliery in Kent, south-east England.

Right: *Stigmaria ficoides,* a fossil root of the giant tree *Lepidodendron,* showing the points where rootlets were attached.

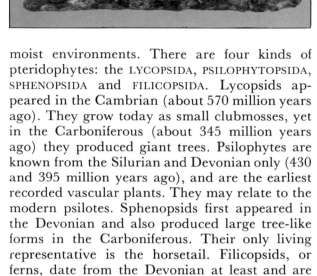

The earliest Pre-Cambrian EUKARYOTES (*see page 6*) were almost certainly green algae. Unlike the blue-green algae from which they evolved, they contain true CHLOROPLASTS and so are seen as ancestors of the higher plants. Modern algae range from single-celled plants to multi-celled seaweeds. As they live in water or damp places they can survive without roots, stems or specialized VASCULAR TISSUES. Some multiply asexually; others reproduce sexually and produce free-swimming gametes.

The more complex BRYOPHYTA, which include MOSSES and LIVERWORTS, are known from Cambrian rocks. They also lack vascular tissues, but do have anchoring RHIZOIDS. Like the algae they are tied to wet or damp sites, and again free-swimming gametes are involved in their reproduction. Although bryophytes seem to represent an intermediate step in the conquest of land by plants, there is no evidence to connect them either with the algae or with more advanced plants.

Plants colonize the land

Adapting to life away from water required that plants develop roots and vascular systems to supply all their parts with food and water. The PTERIDOPHYTA and SPERMATOPHYTA managed to achieve this. Whether they evolved from a common ancestor, or at different times from different non-vascular ancestors, is not clear from the fossil record.

Despite their extra structures the pteridophytes remained associated with wet or damp places as their gametes generally only function in very

Above: A reconstruction of *Lepidodendron,* a lycopsid tree, is shown beside an immature specimen.

Below: A reconstruction of *Medullosa,* a pteridosperm tree about 4 metres high.

moist environments. There are four kinds of pteridophytes: the LYCOPSIDA, PSILOPHYTOPSIDA, SPHENOPSIDA and FILICOPSIDA. Lycopsids appeared in the Cambrian (about 570 million years ago). They grow today as small clubmosses, yet in the Carboniferous (about 345 million years ago) they produced giant trees. Psilophytes are known from the Silurian and Devonian only (430 and 395 million years ago), and are the earliest recorded vascular plants. They may relate to the modern psilotes. Sphenopsids first appeared in the Devonian and also produced large tree-like forms in the Carboniferous. Their only living representative is the horsetail. Filicopsids, or ferns, date from the Devonian at least and are still an important group.

The spermatophytes have no need for moisture to reproduce, as the male gametes form POLLEN grains, and the zygote is protected in a SEED. In one sub-group, the GYMNOSPERMAE, the seeds are partly enclosed, whereas in the other, the ANGIOSPERMAE, the seeds are fully enclosed. From their beginnings in the Devonian, the gymnosperms came to dominate the world's vegetation for much of the Mesozoic, but steadily dwindled after the start of the Cretaceous. Of the various gymnosperms the PTERIDOSPERMALES or seed ferns died out, as did the BENNETTITALES, PENTOXYLALES, and CORDAITALES. Those which survived were the CYCADALES, CONIFERALES, TAXALES, GINKGOALES and GNETALES. Although they may well have an earlier, as yet undetected history, the first fossil angiosperms, or flowering plants, occur in early Cretaceous rock layers. They rapidly colonized the continents and by the

---

a long tube, called a STYLE, which supports a flat POLLEN-receiving surface known as a STIGMA.

Chloroplasts are small bodies containing chlorophyll which occur in the CYTOPLASM (*see page 13*) of a cell. Chlorophyll is a green pigment which traps sunlight and so provides the energy for photosynthesis (*see page 6*).

Coal is made up of partly carbonized vegetable matter and was first formed in swamps. The dead remains of swamp plants accumulated as peat, which on

burial by later sediments was compressed into coal.

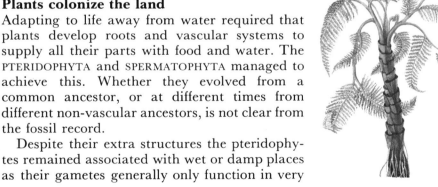

Trees fossilized in coal

Coal swamps were widespread in the northern hemisphere during the Carboniferous.

Coniferopsida are a subdivision of the GYMNOSPERMAE and comprise 4 orders. Of these the CONIFERALES, TAXALES and GINKGOALES have living examples, whereas the CORDAITALES are extinct. The earliest undoubted coniferopsid fossils are of Carboniferous age.

Conifers or Coniferales are an order of the CONIFEROPSIDA.

Cordaitales are an extinct order of the CONIFEROPSIDA.

They first appeared in early Carboniferous times and died out at the end of the Permian. *Cordaites* was an imposing forest tree, at least 30 metres high, with strap-like leaves that were probably tough and leathery in texture.

Cross-fertilization occurs when sex cells or GAMETES (*see page 13*) from 2 organisms fuse to form a ZYGOTE (*see page 15*).

Cuticles consist of a waxy substance called cutin. They cover the leaves and stems of plants and so reduce water loss.

Cycadales are an order of the GYMNOSPERMAE. They first appeared in Upper Triassic times, and flourished during the Jurassic and Cretaceous, though today only 9 cycad GENERA survive. Most of the species resemble palm trees. The group as a whole displays many primitive features, and this is why cycads are often referred to as 'living fossils'.

D **Dichotomous** means dividing into 2. When applied to the branching pattern of the PSILOPSIDA and some members of the LYCOP-

end of the Cretaceous nearly everywhere outnumbered the gymnosperms—a position they have steadily reinforced up to the present day.

Primitive plants

After they emerged in the Lower Palaeozoic, the pteridophytes spread rapidly over the land during the Devonian to form the first forests. By now they were important as food for those animals that were beginning to leave the water. The life-cycle of all pteridophytes involves alternate SPOROPHYTE and GAMETOPHYTE generations. We have already noted how many of these plants were associated with damp habitats because of their gametes. In fact, the gametophytes themselves often only germinate in moist conditions.

Although the earliest pteridophyte fossils are of lycopsids, psilophytes have the most primitive features in the group. They are therefore often seen as the ancestors of the other three, more specialized, sub-groups. If this is true, the groups must have separated into different evolutionary lines in the Cambrian or Ordovician, for each

Above: In this reconstruction the Palaeozoic scene is dominated by lepidodendrids. *Lepidodendron* itself is shown front right, and in front of this is a fallen *Sigillaria* showing a *Stigmaria* root system. Beneath *Lepidodendron* is the small *Proto-lepidodendron,* while another, younger, unbranched specimen of *Lepidodendron* is shown front left. In the distance are several large trees of the genus *Bothodendron.* Numerous ferns are also shown.

sub-group remains distinct as far back as we can trace it. The lack of 'missing links' need not affect this theory, as plants do have a rather poor fossil record. Since they are static, plants are unlikely to be fossilized unless they are already growing in conditions where they may be preserved (such as bogs). They also lack durable hard parts, which makes preservation less likely.

The name psilophyte means 'bare plant', and this is a good description of what it looked like. It had underground structures called RHIZOMES, and from these at intervals arose slender, tapering stems up to 500 millimetres high. The stems were generally leafless and branched in a DICHOTOMOUS manner. Some carried cone-shaped SPORE capsules or SPORANGIA at the top. The stems were solid cylinders and used light to make food in the process which is called PHOTOSYNTHESIS (*see page 9*).

The lycopsids have true leaves and roots. Spore-bearing leaves, or SPOROPHYLLS, differ from the leaves that carry on photosynthesis, though some of the sporophylls may also photosynthesize. The leaves are typically small and scale-like, yet in certain fossil forms they were up to 500 millimetres long and needle-like. The primitive nature of these plants is revealed by the fact that there are no breaks or gaps in the vascular tissue at the point where the leaf bases are attached. The sporangia are often crowded together into a cone or STROBILUS.

The coal forests

Lycopsids dominated the Carboniferous COAL swamps. There were plants resembling their present-day descendants, the clubmosses, as well as the giant trees LEPIDODENDRON and SIGILLARIA. Some specimens of *Lepidodendron* grew up to 30 metres before branching, and were 2 metres across at the base. They branched dichotomously, equally at first but then more unequally. The root system had four large branches which also divided dichotomously. Fossils of these roots are named STIGMARIA. Long grass-like leaves were bunched towards the ends of the smallest branches. When these leaves dropped off, diamond-shaped scars were left, even on the oldest wood. *Sigillaria* had similar scars, but these were arranged in vertical rows and were round, hexagonal or oval in shape. The cones of *Lepidodendron* were up to 750 millimetres long and

SIDA, it refers to the Y-shaped forking of their stems.
Dicotyledons are 1 of the 2 classes of ANGIOSPERMAE. Their name derives from the fact that they have 2 seed leaves, or cotyledons, instead of the one in MONO-COTYLEDONS. The leaves of dicotyledons are generally broader and have a network of veins, whereas those of monocotyledons are long and thin and they have veins that run parallel to each other.
Disjunct distributions of plants or animals are those where the geographical

ranges of the organisms concerned are broken up into distinct areas. These areas are separated by distance or environment (or both) and cannot be bridged by any of the organisms' methods of dispersal. The term 'disjunct' can be applied to species, GENERA or FAMILIES.

E Endemic groups of plants or animals are those which have a very restricted geographical range. The term 'endemic' may be applied to species, GENERA or FAMILIES.

Equisetum is the only surviving genus (see GENERA) of the SPHENOPSIDA. It includes all the horsetails, which are plants of damp places. The stems of horsetails are jointed, and at each joint there is a ring of small branches.

F Families are groupings used in classifying plants and animals. Related GENERA make up a family, and related families make up an order.
Fertilize is a term used when describing reproduction in organisms. It refers to

Fossil fern, Alethopteris serli

hung from the ends of some smaller branches. The air wherever these trees and their allies grew in numbers must at times have been filled with spores from these strobili. Some interesting features are found in the fossil cone known as *Lepidocarpon*. There is only one functional MEGAS-PORE in each sporangium, which in turn is almost completely enveloped by the sporophyll. Such an arrangement strongly resembles a true seed, and may provide a hint as to how seeds originated. *Lepidodendron* and its allies adapted to a life in swamps by having plenty of tissues for the exchange of gases, but few for conducting water. This probably explains why they apparently failed to adapt to climatic changes after the Carboniferous.

The sphenopsids also flourished in the Carboniferous coal swamps. These plants have true roots, stems and primitive leaves. Their stems are generally jointed and the leaves grow in whorls around the joints or nodes. True branch and leaf gaps seem not to occur in the vascular tissues. In many fossil sphenopsids the sporangia were developed into strobili, as they are in the living examples. Whereas the lycopsids that survive include a thousand species in many GENERA and several FAMILIES, the only surviving sphenopsid genus is EQUISETUM, with 24 or 25 species. Of the fossil groups, CALAMITES, which was closely related to *Equisetum*, included tree-like forms that grew 20–30 metres. The various types of *Calamites* carried their cones in different positions. Some were borne in clusters at the

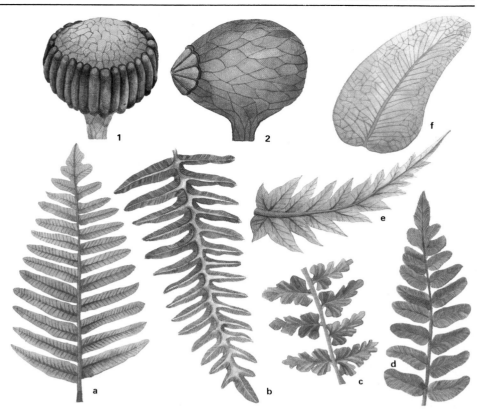

Above: The Carboniferous fern-like leaves shown are:
(**a**) *Pecopteris,*
(**b**) *Alethopteris,*
(**c**) *Sphenopteris,*
(**d**) *Neuropteris,*
(**e**) *Mariopteris,*
(**f**) *Linopteris.* Also shown are the sporangia of living ferns, (**1**) *Gleichenia* and (**2**) *Lygodium.* Ferns are classified largely according to the structure of the sporangium.

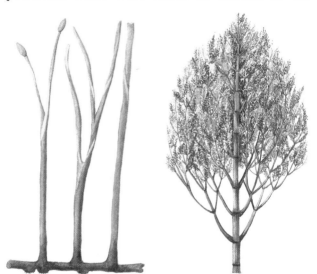

Far left: A reconstruction of the psilophyte *Rhynia* shows the simplest vascular plant so far recorded.

Left: A reconstruction of the sphenopsid tree *Calamites*.

ends of the smaller branches; others hung singly from the nodes, or grew on specialized branches. *Calamites* fossils are plentiful in Carboniferous rocks, internal casts of the stem being most common. Fossils of the leaf whorls are of two types. ASTEROPHYLLITES are those in which the leaves are needle-like; those in which the leaves are more oval are called ANNULARIA.

Filicopsids are the most numerous pteridophytes. They have roots, stems, and large leaves that probably evolved from systems of branches. Apart from large leaves, filicopsids also differ from other pteridophytes as they have leaf and branch gaps that interrupt the cylinder of vascular tissues. In this they are like the gymnosperms and angiosperms. The sporangia vary, as do their positions on the leaves.

Fossil ferns are very diverse, with some huge tree-like types known from the Palaeozoic. So numerous are fossils of ferns and fern-like foliage from the Carboniferous that geologists once called it the 'Age of Ferns'. We now realize that some of these 'ferns' belonged to the seed ferns, an extinct group of gymnosperms.

---

the fusion of 2 gametes to form a ZYGOTE (*see page 15*).
Filicopsida are a subdivision of the PTERIDOPHYTA and include all living and extinct ferns. The earliest ferns are known from rocks of Devonian age.
Flora refers to all the plant species in a given area. In contrast, 'vegetation' may be defined as the kind of plant cover in an area (for example, forest or grassland).
Flower is the reproductive structure in the ANGIOSPERMAE or flowering plants. It forms a receptacle which supports

4 sets of organs. The first is an outer ring of sepals, normally green. Inside these are petals, frequently brightly coloured so as to attract insects. Within the petals occur the male and female sex organs — these are the STAMENS and CARPELS respectively.

G Gametophyte is that stage in the life cycle of a plant when sex cells, or gametes, are produced. In BRYOPHYTA the gametophyte forms the adult plant, but in most PTERIDOPHYTA the gametophyte is only a small

PROTHALLUS, unimportant compared to the SPOROPHYTE (or spore-producing) generation. In advanced pteridophytes there is no free-living prothallus. Instead spores of differing size are produced. A male prothallus develops inside the MICROSPORE and a female prothallus inside the MEGAS-PORE. This is taken a stage further in SPERMATOPHYTA, where the male gametophyte is the POLLEN grain and the female occurs in the OVULE.
Genera is the plural for genus. A genus is made up of related species, so *Erica*

Maidenhair leaves

cinerea and *Erica tetralix* are both species of heather belonging to the same genus, *Erica*.
Ginkgoales are an order of the GYMNOSPERMAE. There is only one surviving species — *Ginkgo biloba* — the Maidenhair tree. Fossil leaves identical to those of *Ginkgo biloba* are found in Triassic rocks 200 million years old.
Gnetales are an order of the GYMNOSPERMAE. They have few fossil remains and consist of just 3 GENERA.
Gnetopsida are a subdivision of the GYMNOSPERMAE

Gymnosperms

Gymnosperms differ from pteridophytes in having a true seed, which derived from the MEGASPORANGIUM in advanced pteridophytes. To explain how, we must look at the trend from HOMOSPORY to HETEROSPORY as shown in pteridophyte fossils during the Devonian.

Homospory is the production of spores of one size. These grow into free-living gametophytes, and each gametophyte or PROTHALLUS gives rise to male and female gametes. The male gamete swims in a film of moisture to the female gamete, with which it fuses to form a zygote. The next sporophyte generation then develops from the zygote. CROSS-FERTILIZATION can only occur if there is enough moisture for the male gamete to swim from one prothallus to another. In heterospory the spores are of two sizes— MICROSPORES and megaspores—which respec-

tively will germinate into male and female gametophytes. They grow inside the spores while these are in the sporangia, and on different prothalli. The megaspores, being heavier, fall near the parent plant and rupture to reveal the female prothallus. The microspores are produced in greater numbers and are carried away by air currents, so that they can FERTILIZE the megaspores of other plants. Heterospory therefore allows cross-fertilization to occur even in relatively dry places.

Gymnosperms are also heterosporous. But the megaspore with its female gamete is kept in the megasporangium, which stays attached to the plant. Tissue grows around the megasporangium and together they form an OVULE, which becomes a seed at maturity. The microspores contain the male gametophytes which are now called pollen. They are carried by the wind to an

Above: This reconstruction of a frond of the Permian seed fern *Emplectopteris* also shows the seeds.

Left: (**1**) A reconstruction of *Williamsonia sewordiana,* a representative of the extinct Bennettitales. (**4**) is a living cycad tree, (**5**) a cycad cone and (**2**) and (**3**) show some of the problems in reconstructing fossil plants. (**2**) is the fossil cone, *Cycadeoidea,* of the Bennettitales. It is often shown unfurled as in (**3**), but no such opened cones have ever actually been seen.

and comprise one order, the GNETALES.
Gondwana was an ancient southern continent which broke up in the Mesozoic to give South America, Africa, India, Australia and Antarctica.
Gymnospermae are a subdivision of the SPERMATOPHYTA. The OVULES of gymnosperms are carried 'naked' on cone-scales; in the ANGIOSPERMAE they are enclosed in an OVARY.

H Heterospory occurs in advanced members of the PTERIDOPHYTA. It involves

producing spores of different size — a MEGASPORE and a MICROSPORE. Microspores are carried farther from the parent plant than the heavier megaspores, so microspores of one plant FERTILIZE the spores of another. When a microspore lands on a ruptured megaspore, fertilization can take place, even in fairly dry conditions. Heterospory therefore allows CROSS-FERTILIZATION, and enables heterosporous pteridophytes to live in a wider range of habitats than homosporous types.
Homospory involves plants

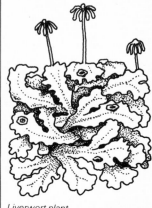

Liverwort plant

producing spores of the same size. In homosporous PTERIDOPHYTA, a spore develops into a GAMETOPHYTE — the PROTHALLUS — on which both the male and female sex cells are produced. The prothallus and male sex cells can only function where there is enough moisture. So homosporous pteridophytes are tied to damp places.

L Laurasia was an ancient northern continent which broke up in late Mesozoic times to give North America and Eurasia.
Lepidodendron is a type of

fossil LYCOPSIDA found in Carboniferous rocks. They were trees, some of which grew over 30 metres high. Fossils of the outside trunk or branches show diamond-shaped leaf-scars.
Liverworts are a class of BRYOPHYTA.
Lycopsida are a subdivision of the PTERIDOPHYTA. Living examples are the clubmosses.

M Megasporangium is a structure which is found in advanced PTERIDOPHYTA. When ripe, it releases MEGASPORES.

opening in the ovule, and fertilization occurs inside. In effect, the seed is a protected zygote.

Although gymnosperms are known from the Devonian and were well established in the late Carboniferous, they replaced pteridophytes as the main plant types only in the Permian, after lycopsid and sphenopsid trees became extinct. We have noted already that the lycopsid trees at least may have died out owing to climatic change. Significantly, one group of gymnosperms dating from the late Carboniferous are the CONIFERS. Many of these have needle-leaves and thick CUTICLES, both adaptations for reducing moisture loss. This suggests that the climatic change was towards greater aridity.

The gymnosperms fall into three groups: the Cycadopsida, CONIFEROPSIDA and GNETOPSIDA. The last group has a limited fossil record and is made up of the Gnetales only. These are remarkable plants including trees, shrubs, lianes and turnip-like plants. Typical cycadopsids have large frond-like leaves, while the coniferopsids have needle-, fan- or paddle-shaped leaves. Both groups appear more or less at the same time in the Devonian. The earliest cycadopsids were the seed ferns, or pteridosperms, some of which grew like small trees, up to 5 metres high. Despite having seeds, the pteridosperms died out in the Cretaceous. Before they disappeared they were joined by three other types of cycadopsids: the cycads, Bennettitales and Pentoxylales. Of these only the cycads managed to survive until the present, as evolutionary relics. The Bennettitales resembled the cycads and had structures that looked more like flowers than cones.

The earliest coniferopsids were the Cordaitales — tall, slender trees over 30 metres tall, with a crown of paddle-shaped leaves. After they died out in the Permian, they were replaced by the ginkgos and conifers, two other types of coniferopsids. Just one kind of ginkgo — the maidenhair tree — now survives, and has been described as a living fossil. Conifers are still numerous, but are not so widely distributed today. The same is true of the youngest coniferopsids, the Taxales or yews.

Angiosperms

Angiosperms are the most advanced plants and as such are the equivalent of the mammals in the animal kingdom. Although they bear seeds,

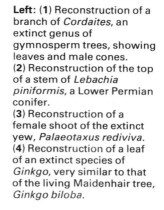

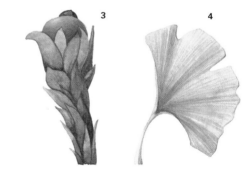

Left: (1) Reconstruction of a branch of *Cordaites*, an extinct genus of gymnosperm trees, showing leaves and male cones. (2) Reconstruction of the top of a stem of *Lebachia piniformis*, a Lower Permian conifer. (3) Reconstruction of a female shoot of the extinct yew, *Palaeotaxus rediviva*. (4) Reconstruction of a leaf of an extinct species of *Ginkgo*, very similar to that of the living Maidenhair tree, *Ginkgo biloba*.

Megaspore is the spore which in higher plants divides to produce the female GAMETOPHYTE generation.
Megasporophyll is the special, modified leaf which bears the MEGASPORANGIUM.
Microspores are produced by plants belonging to the advanced PTERIDOPHYTA. A male GAMETOPHYTE develops inside the microspore, which can be carried great distances by air currents.
Monocotyledons are 1 of the 2 classes of ANGIOSPERMAE. See DICOTYLEDONS.
Mosses are a class of BRYOPHYTA.

Clubmoss

N **Niches** are environmental 'slots'. In each 'slot' a population of one organism fills a specific role within its surroundings, and follows a particular way of life.

O **Ovary** is the structure which contains one or more OVULES.
Ovules contain the female sex cells. A single female sex cell, or egg cell, is called an ovum.

P **Pentoxylales** are an extinct order of the GYMNOSPERMAE. They lived in Jurassic times and were shrubs or small trees.
Pollen grains contain the male sex cells of the SPER-

Fossil pollen spore

MATOPHYTA. They correspond to, and evolved from, the MICROSPORES of some PTERIDOPHYTA.
Prothallus is another name for GAMETOPHYTE. Passing from the lowly BRYOPHYTA through the PTERIDOPHYTA to the advanced SPERMATOPHYTA, the prothallus becomes progressively more unimportant. In bryophytes the prothallus is the adult plant; in many pteridophytes it is reduced to a small green plant, independent of the larger SPOROPHYTE generation. In higher pteridophytes there are no free-living or

Left: Fossil leaves very like this leaf of the tulip tree, *Liriodendron*, are well known from rocks of the Cretaceous period. *Liriodendron* belongs to the Magnolia family, which is regarded as the most primitive of living angiosperms. By late Cretaceous times, leaf impressions of angiosperms are plentiful in the fossil record. Many of the fossil leaves found closely resemble those of living angiosperms.

Right: A selection of fossil seeds and fruit from the Eocene London Clay: (**1**) worn fruit with seeds; (**4**) fruit; (**3**) internal cast of seed of the stemless palm *Nipa*; (**5**) internal cast of seed; and (**2**) a locule cast. Although the fruits and seeds which make up the London Clay flora were clearly carried out to sea, it is unlikely that they were conveyed any great distance by oceanic currents. In the first place the fossils are so abundant, and in the second very few of them show any structural adaptations for floating over long periods of time in ocean currents. Lastly, although modern beach drift may contain some far-travelled seeds and fruits, it is mainly of local origin.

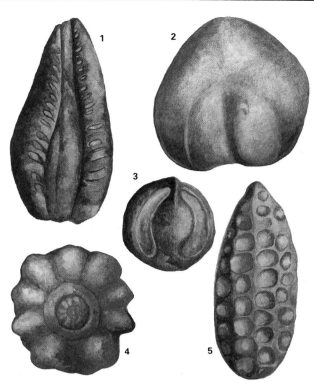

Right: This fossil of a palm-like leaf, *Sanmiguela lewisi*, has been suggested as being of a true palm. However, it is preserved in mid-Triassic rocks, and its acceptance as a fossil palm is therefore by no means widely accepted. The oldest undoubted angiosperms are known from Lower Cretaceous rocks.

angiosperms have several features which make them different from gymnosperms. First, the ovules are encased in an OVARY, and the seed grows inside a fruit developed from the ovary. Also, the structures bearing pollen are modified into STAMENS, and those carrying ovules into CARPELS. Both are inside a FLOWER, instead of the cone of pteridophytes and gymnosperms. Unlike the gymnosperm ovule, the carpel is closed and the pollen grains germinate on a sticky surface or STIGMA. On germination a tube extends from the pollen grain down through a cylinder called a STYLE and fuses with the female gamete in the ovule.

Efficient reproduction and seed dispersal are partly the reasons for the great success of the angiosperms. The closed carpel allows the ovule to be fertilized at a very early stage, and also to be discarded without waste if fertilization does not occur. The carpel probably began as a MEGASPOROPHYLL that remained closed, protecting the megasporangium and megaspore, and ultimately the seed. In the same way, the stamen would have been a sporophyll carrying microsporangia, and these were later covered by the tissue of an anther.

The development of colourful, scented flowers represents a further advance. The insects, birds and bats which they attract transfer pollen economically from one plant to another. Animal-pollinated plants therefore produce relatively little pollen, while wind-pollinated plants have to release clouds of it to ensure pollination. However, some angiosperms reverted to pollination by wind, apparently in places where animals could not be relied upon to perform the task. After flowers come fruits, which are adaptations that favour seed dispersal. Fruits with wings are carried by wind, pods explode and scatter seeds, while fruits such as berries or nuts, or those with fleshy coverings, are dispersed by animals.

Angiosperms throughout the world
The ancestors and precise beginnings of the angiosperms are not clearly known. When they first appear in Lower Cretaceous rocks they already show some variety and the two major angiosperm classes — DICOTYLEDONS and MONOCOTYLEDONS — are represented as well. So it seems that they must have begun earlier, in Permian or Triassic times, in tropical uplands where conditions would not have favoured

plant prothalli. Instead a male prothallus develops inside a MICROSPORE and a female inside a MEGASPORE. In spermatophytes, the male and female prothalli (or what remains of them) are found in POLLEN grains and OVULES respectively.
Psilophytopsida are an extinct sub-division of the PTERIDOPHYTA, with fossils found only in Silurian and Devonian rocks.
Psilopsida are a group of 4 plant species, native to the tropics and sub-tropics. Best known is the whisk 'fern' *Psilotum*.

Pteridophyta are a division of the plant kingdom. They include the LYCOPSIDA, SPHENOPSIDA, FILICOPSIDA, psilotopsida and the extinct PSILOPHYTOPSIDA. Pteridophytes produce SPORES.
Pteridospermales are an extinct order of GYMNOSPERMAE. They were seed ferns.

R **Rhizoids** are tiny root-like threads which attach MOSSES and LIVERWORTS to the ground.
Rhizome is a modified stem which grows horizontally underground, and serves as a food-store.

S **Seed** is a fertilized OVULE enclosed in a protective coat. A seed gives rise to a larger plant than does the SPORE of lower plants because it contains a reserve of food.
Sigillaria is a genus (see GENERA) of fossil lycopsids

Rhizomes of water mint

found in Carboniferous and Permian rocks. *Sigillaria* trees were common in the Carboniferous coal-swamps and impressions of their trunks show squarish leaf-scars arranged in vertical rows.
Spermatophyta are a divi-

sion of the plant kingdom. They are seed-bearing plants which are sub-divided into the GYMNOSPERMAE and ANGIOSPERMAE, or flowering plants.
Sphenopsida are a sub-division of the PTERIDOPHYTA. In Carboniferous times they were numerous, producing tree-like forms. Their only living examples are the horsetails, which are grouped into a single genus, EQUISETUM.
Sporangia are the SPORE-containing structures of the algae, BRYOPHYTA and PTERIDOPHYTA.

apart by the end of the Cretaceous. Evidently many angiosperm families had spread throughout Gondwana before the break-up was complete. Some angiosperm genera must also have existed before the break-up, as they occur on several Gondwana fragments. For example, the southern beeches, *Nothofagus*, are DISJUNCT between South America, south-east Australia, Tasmania and New Zealand. And the baobab trees, *Adansonia*, are found in East Africa, Madagascar and Australia.

The angiosperms continued to evolve on their different landmasses until there are now about 225,000 species. They range in size from floating duckweeds to towering trees, and have adapted to a vast array of habitats and NICHES. As they developed isolated from each other, some angiosperms underwent convergent evolution. That is, they grew to look alike while adapting to the same basic way of life. Cacti, for instance, evolved in drier regions of the New World, while euphorbias exploited the same type of habitat in the Old World. Physical resemblances between these two groups are very striking.

fossilization. But recent research on fossil pollen suggests that the amount of time required for angiosperm development in the pre-Cretaceous has probably been much exaggerated.

It is clear, however, that the angiosperms achieved near-global dominance over other plants by the end of the Cretaceous. Almost everywhere today the same four angiosperm families — daisies, grasses, peas and sedges — are among the six most numerous. From this it also follows that there is no unique or ENDEMIC angiosperm FLORA, even in the isolated southern continents of Australia and South America.

This even distribution of angiosperms could not have happened so quickly if the continents had always been in their present positions, separated as they are by huge oceans. But we know that in the Cretaceous, when the angiosperms were evolving, the landmasses were still grouped into two super-continents, LAURASIA in the north and GONDWANA in the south. They were separated by the ancient TETHYS ocean, the shrunken remnant of which is today the Mediterranean Sea. The continental fragments of Laurasia are still in contact or nearly so, but those which made up Gondwana had drifted

Above: A fossil leaf from a flowering plant found in rocks of the Eocene period, London Clay age. It can be seen that this leaf strongly resembles one from the kind of broad-leaved, hardwood trees living today.

Below: Developing in isolation of each other, some angiosperms underwent convergent evolution. That is, they grew to look alike in the process of adapting to the same basic way of life. Cacti, for instance, evolved in the drier regions of the New World, while euphorbias exploited the same habitat in the Old World. The physical resemblances between these 2 groups are now often very striking.

Cactus   Euphorbia

Spore is a structure involved in the reproductive processes of many plants. In some PTERIDOPHYTA the spore develops into a PROTHALLUS; in others separate spores carry the male and female sex cells.

Sporophylls carry SPORANGIA and are normally modified leaves.

Sporophyte is the SPORE-bearing generation in the life-cycle of a plant.

Stamens are filaments which support the POLLEN-sacs (or anthers) in flowering plants. They probably derived from SPOROPHYLLS.

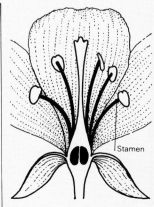

Flower stamens

Stamen

Stigma is a plant's flat POLLEN-receiving surface (see CARPEL).

Stigmaria are fossil roots of the extinct LEPIDODENDRON. They grew more or less horizontally and forked into 2 (see DICHOTOMOUS). The former positions of RHIZOIDS are marked by round scars on the fossil roots.

Strobilus is another name for a cone, which is a structure made up of SPOROPHYLLS. Various PTERIDOPHYTA have strobili which carry SPORES. Cones of the GYMNOSPERMAE carry POLLEN and OVULES.

Style, see CARPEL.

Taxales are an order of the GYMNOSPERMAE which includes the yews. They differ from conifers in having a single OVULE, which is not on a cone-scale, and which is surrounded when ripe by a fleshy structure rather like a berry. They are the youngest of the CONIFEROPSIDA, entering the fossil record in late Cretaceous times.

Tethys was an ancient seaway connecting the Atlantic and Indian oceans, and separating the former super-continents of LAURASIA and GONDWANA. The Mediterranean Sea is its remnant.

Vascular tissue is organized into phloem, which conducts food and other materials up and down inside the plant, and xylem, which conducts water and minerals. Non-vascular plants include MOSSES, LIVERWORTS, algae and lichens.

The numerous basic forms of animals without backbones represent different lines of experiment in evolution. Many have survived, with varying success, to the present day.

Evolution of Invertebrates

The first animals appeared on Earth about 800 million years ago. They probably came from eukaryotic sea-living algae, but unlike their ancestors, they lacked CHLOROPLASTS (*see page 17*). The earliest animals were single-celled and both they and their living examples are grouped under the PROTOZOA. From simple beginnings the protozoans evolved many elaborate forms, and some developed skeletons for support and protection. Protozoans are the founder members of the animal family tree and the simplest of all the animals without backbones — the INVERTEBRATES.

In time, protozoans probably grouped together to form cell clumps, each type of cell specializing to perform a particular task. These clumps, or aggregates, were the first step towards multi-celled organisms and they probably looked like very simple SPONGES. Sponges are themselves the simplest multi-celled animals, each one being made up of a small variety of cells. These cells are organized into layers but are not grouped to form tissues as they are in the METAZOANS, which are higher invertebrates. Sponges are mostly FILTER-FEEDERS, drawing food into a large central body cavity through numerous tiny pores. The body is often supported by needle-like SPICULES, which may be of calcite, silica or a horny material called spongin. The spicules can be single units or may be fused together in a rigid framework. Evolutionary trends among the sponges are difficult to pick out, but there are several grades of organization which show the creatures becoming more complex. The simplest sponges (ASCON-GRADE) have a sac-like body but in others there is a folding and refolding of the

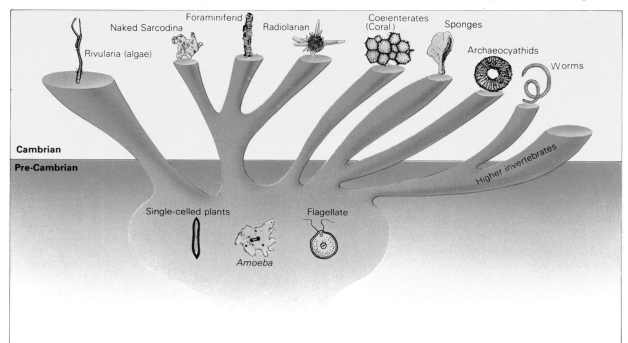

Cambrian

Pre-Cambrian

Rivularia (algae) · Naked Sarcodina · Foraminiferid · Radiolarian · Coelenterates (Coral) · Sponges · Archaeocyathids · Worms · Higher invertebrates · Single-celled plants · Flagellate · Amoeba

Left: Life began in the seas of the Pre-Cambrian when single-celled plants originated from non-living matter. Approximately 800 million years ago they were joined by the first single-celled animals, such as *Amoeba*, from which arose a host of different living creatures, including the sponges, corals and archaeocyathids.

Reference

A **Acorn worms** are a group of HEMICHORDATES and therefore linked directly with GRAPTOLITES.

Ammonites were the most important CEPHALOPODS of the Mesozoic. Although most were PLANISPIRAL, some were either loosely or spirally coiled. Most have complex SUTURE LINES. The ammonites are important ZONE (*see page 11*) fossils for both the Jurassic and Cretaceous periods.

Ammonoids are an extinct group of CEPHALOPOD MOLLUSCS with SUTURE LINES varying from gently folded to complex. Most are PLANISPIRAL. The sub-class includes GONIATITES, CERATITES and AMMONITES.

Anisograptidae are an important family of GRAPTOLITES with characters that fall between those of the DENDROIDS and the GRAPTOLOIDS. They are known only from the Lower Ordovician.

Annelid worm is a segmented soft-bodied animal. The general term 'annelid' applies to all earthworms, sandworms and leeches.

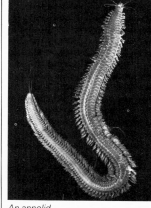

An annelid

Anthozoa are sea-bottom dwelling COELENTERATES with POLYPOID adults. They include the TABULATE corals and the RUGOSE and SCLERACTINIAN corals.

Archaeocyathids are an extinct INVERTEBRATE group with similarities to SPONGES. They may have lived in SYMBIOSIS with some TRILOBITES.

Archaeogastropods are a primitive group of GASTROPODS with 2 gills. The common limpet, *Patella vulgata*, is a living example of this group, which first appeared in the Cambrian.

Arthropods are INVERTEBRATES with a segmented body and jointed legs. They have an EXOSKELETON of a horny material called chitin. Various water, land and aerial types are known. Fossil forms include the TRILOBITES and EURYPTERIDS, while living insects, butterflies and spiders are among the most common invertebrates.

Ascon grade describes the sac-like form which is the simplest structure among SPONGES.

B **Belemnoids**, or belemnites, are an extinct

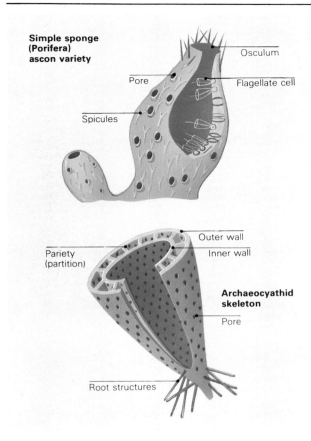

Simple sponge (Porifera) ascon variety

Osculum
Pore
Flagellate cell
Spicules

Pariety (partition)
Outer wall
Inner wall

Archaeocyathid skeleton
Pore

Root structures

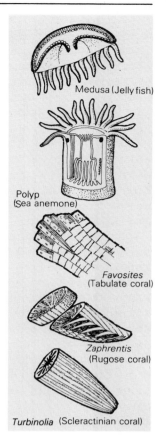

Medusa (Jelly fish)

Polyp (Sea anemone)

Favosites (Tabulate coral)

Zaphrentis (Rugose coral)

Turbinolia (Scleractinian coral)

Above (top): A simple sponge showing both pores and 3-pronged spicules. The illustration is drawn in section to show the large inner cavity and upper opening. Water is taken in by the sponge through the pores and forced out again through the top opening. **(Bottom):** A sketch of an archaeocyathid. Most of these animals had a double-walled structure and pores like the sponges. Archaeocyathids were reef-forming animals, but little is known of their soft parts.

Above: The jellyfish and sea anemone are living representatives of the coelenterates. The jellyfish is a free-living animal, but polyps of the sea anemone live attached to the sea floor. Tabulate corals flourished during the Silurian and Devonian periods. All lived in colonies, with some form of connection existing between the soft parts of each individual. Tabulates died out at the end of the Permian. Rugose corals were probably the dominant coelenterates of the Upper Palaeozoic. Their skeletons were more complex than those of their tabulate cousins, and their soft parts were probably also more advanced in evolution. Scleractinian corals first appeared in the Middle Triassic, probably deriving from a rugosan ancestor. They are important in reef communities today.

Cambrian is one of the mysteries of fossil history, and their place as reef-builders remained vacant for tens of millions of years.

Coelenterates

The JELLYFISH and SEA ANEMONES in the seas of the world are soft-bodied creatures which show a higher level of evolution than either the sponges or the archaeocyathids. Both belong to the COELENTERATES. Jellyfish are the free-swimming MEDUSOID type and sea anemones the fixed POLYPOID type. Each has a long geological record, as the first jellyfish and the first sea-pens (ANTHOZOA-alcyonarian corals) come from rocks in Australia which are dated to about 690 million years old.

These discoveries prove that the coelenterate group is one of the most ancient metazoan lines, but only from the Middle Ordovician onwards can we follow a detailed record of important evolutionary trends. At this time appeared the TABULATE and RUGOSE CORALS (Anthozoa-Zoantharia), which had calcareous hard parts. We can compare these to the beautiful skeletons of living SCLERACTINIAN corals which are secreted by soft tissues at the base of the polyp. The tabulates were the simplest of the coral groups mentioned, as they lacked the complex inner structures of the others. They lived only in colonies and reached their peak during the Silurian and Devonian periods. The thin horizontal plates known as tabulae are their most recognizable feature, and the most important evolutionary trends they developed were pores in their connecting walls and dense tissue between the cups or corallites. Remains of rugose corals living in colonies appear later than solitary ones, and we generally think of colonial animals as being more advanced. However, both types show evolutionary trends linked with skeletal features such as the tabulae. Some trends can be linked to major phases in the evolution of the rugose corals, and a few seem to have been adopted by the scleractinian corals from the Triassic onwards. By reconstructing the soft parts of extinct tabulates and rugosans, we can tell that they were less advanced than the scleractinians. All three corals may be linked in one evolutionary line, but it is more likely that each arose independently from a soft-bodied, anemone-like ancestor.

body wall which produces a much more complex structure.

Sponges have lived since the Pre-Cambrian and their long fossil history contrasts with that of their distant cousins the ARCHAEOCYATHIDS. These are known only from the Cambrian and present problems, as they have similarities to both the sponges and the corals. Like sponges they had pores, but their overall structure was more complex and some people have seen them as being more advanced (albeit short-lived) multi-celled organisms. The archaeocyathids were the first animals to form reefs and they may have lived side by side with TRILOBITES, in SYMBIOSIS. Their demise during the Middle

---

Water spider, an arthropod

group of DIBRANCHIATE cephalopod MOLLUSCS. They are first recorded from the Lower Carboniferous but became really important only in the Jurassic. They were probably the ancestors of the living cuttlefish *Sepia*.
Benthic comes from *benthos*, 'bottom dwellers', and describes creatures that live on or in sea-floor sediments. They include scavengers – which consume carcasses or carrion – as well as creatures that feed by filtering organic debris from seawater or sea-floor sediments.
Bilateral symmetry is

where one side or half of an animal is the mirror-image of the other.
Bivalves are soft-bodied MOLLUSCS with oval or elongated shells comprising 2 hinged valves. They first appeared during the Cambrian. Today their roles are as burrowing, boring, fixed and free-living animals.
Brachiopods are solitary INVERTEBRATES living at the sea bottom. Their soft parts are enclosed in a 2-valved shell. Superficially they resemble the bivalves but have a different size and form. The group is divided into the

INARTICULATES and the articulates – both of which arose in the Cambrian.
Bryozoans are a little known but important group of COELOMATES. They live in colonies and have a skeleton made up of minute box-like units. First known from the Cambrian, they thrive today in many areas.
Burgess shales are fine-grained rocks in the Mount Field district of British Columbia, Canada, renowned for their fossils.
Byssus is a thread-like structure used by certain BIVALVES as a holdfast. It is

secreted as a thick fluid which hardens on contact with seawater.

C **Centipedes** are ARTHROPODS with flattened, segmented bodies, each segment having a pair of limbs. They appear in the Upper Carboniferous.
Cephalopods are close relatives of the gastropods and BIVALVES and are members of the MOLLUSC family. They are marine animals with the single-valved shell divided by septa. They range from the Cambrian to Recent periods.

Bryozoans and brachiopods

The small, often delicate moss animals, BRYO-ZOANS, and the sea-shells called BRACHIOPODS are usually grouped under the heading of minor COELOMATES. This means that they both have an internal cavity, or coelom, which houses the gut, and that they probably arose from the same ancestor. A likely forebear was a PHORONID WORM, a soft-bodied animal that had filaments around the mouth for feeding. This creature dwelt in the soft muds of the sea floor, and so the origin of both bryozoans and brachiopods involved them changing to a SEDIMENT SURFACE-DWELLING way of life.

The first brachiopods probably lacked hard parts, but forms with mineralized skeletons had appeared by the early Cambrian. From then on we have enough evidence to record the numerous RADIATIONS that have taken place during the last 570 million years of geological time. The first involved the least specialized brachiopods — the INARTICULATES. These forms have a phosphatic skeleton and a complex arrangement of muscles to control opening of the two valves. LINGULA is a living example of the inarticulates and the diagram shows that it also lacks an inner skeleton. The inarticulates flourished in the Cambrian but by the Ordovician they had been overtaken by forms with a calcareous shell. At first these were small and had no inner structures for support, but in time some grew to enormous sizes and developed complex skeletons to support the organ used for feeding (the lophophore). These articulate brachiopods, as they are called, flourished during the Palaeozoic and Mesozoic, occupying many niches in both shallow and deep water environments. Among the best-known articulates are RHYNCHONELLA, PRODUCTUS, TEREBRATULA and SPIRIFER.

The bryozoans are first known from the Ordovician and in contrast to their brachiopod cousins they all lived in colonies. They have undergone several great radiations during the last 500 million years and played important roles as reef-building animals. During the Palaeozoic the most important group was the TREPOSTOMES or 'stony bryozoans', several of which grew to 500 millimetres across. In the Mesozoic the CHEILOSTOMES became the most successful of all bryozoans. They developed complex front wall structures and many individuals in the colony

Right: Tens of thousands of brachiopods are known from geological records. They first appeared in the Cambrian in the form of inarticulates, which probably gave rise to a host of articulate families. Inarticulates have a rather simple shell consisting of 2 valves. The articulate shell is also made of 2 valves but many types have internal support structures. The diagram shows the relative importance of different brachiopod stocks through time.

a – Obellids
b – Paterinids
c – Kutorginids

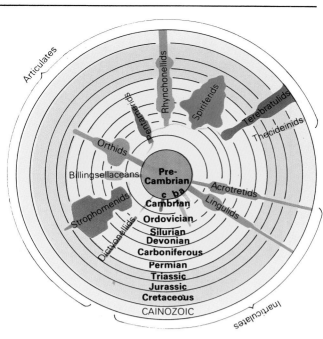

From 'Treatise on Invertebrate Paleontology', courtesy of the Geological Society of America and University of Kansas.

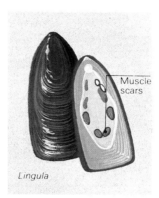
Lingula
Muscle scars

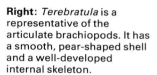
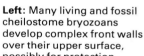
Front walls of living cheilostome bryozoans

Terebratula

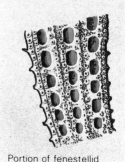
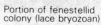
Portion of fenestellid colony (lace bryozoan)

Left: *Lingula,* an inarticulate brachiopod, has survived since the Ordovician. The inside of the shell is marked by a number of well-defined muscle scars.

Right: *Terebratula* is a representative of the articulate brachiopods. It has a smooth, pear-shaped shell and a well-developed internal skeleton.

Left: Many living and fossil cheilostome bryozoans develop complex front walls over their upper surface, possibly for protection.

Right: The many-branched colonies of the fenestellid or 'window bryozoans' are common in Upper Palaeozoic sediments.

Ceratites are AMMONOIDS in which the backward-directed lobes of the SUTURE LINE are frilled. They are found mainly from the Triassic.
Cheilostomes are the major group of living BRYO-ZOANS. They first appear in the Jurassic.
Chordates are animals which have a rod of flexible tissue — the notochord — or, in more advanced forms, a backbone. The notochord was probably the first support structure to evolve in vertebrate ancestors.
Coelenterates are the sim-plest METAZOANS with 2 layers

of cells (tissues) in the body wall. They are first known from the late Pre-Cambrian.
Coelomate animals include all those above the COELENT-ERATE METAZOANS. In coelo-mates there are 3 layers of cells (tissues) of which the outer layer forms the skin and the inner layer the gut. All higher INVERTEBRATES and vertebrates have a fluid-filled cavity — the coelom.
Corals are marine COELENT-ERATES which have a POLYPOID adult form. They have exter-nal skeletons which may be solitary or compound.
Crustaceans are mainly

water-living ARTHROPODS which show great variation in their limb structure. They include barnacles, crabs and lobsters.
Cuttlefish are living CEPHALOPODS. They have 10 arms and their shell is a small internal structure.

D Dendroids are an ex-tinct group of HEMICHOR-DATES and an important order of the GRAPTOLITES, with many branches and 2 types of THECAL CUP on the outside of each branch. They ranged from the mid-Cambrian to the Carboniferous.

Deposit-feeders swallow up mud and organic material from the sea floor. Much of the mud they take in is deposited as casts.

A cuttlefish

Dibranchiates are those CEPHALOPOD MOLLUSCS with 2 gills, such as octopuses. Dib-ranchiates are first recorded from the Carboniferous.

Venus (shallow burrower)

Siphon

Mya (deep burrower)

Mytilus (attached)

Byssus

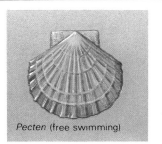

Pecten (free swimming)

Left: Bivalve shells reflect the animal's way of life. Shallow burrowers (*Venus*) have short symmetrical valves. Deep burrowers (*Mya*) are elongate. Attached forms (*Mytilus*) are elongate with a flat lower surface for stability. Free-living forms (*Pecten*) take the shape of their muscles.

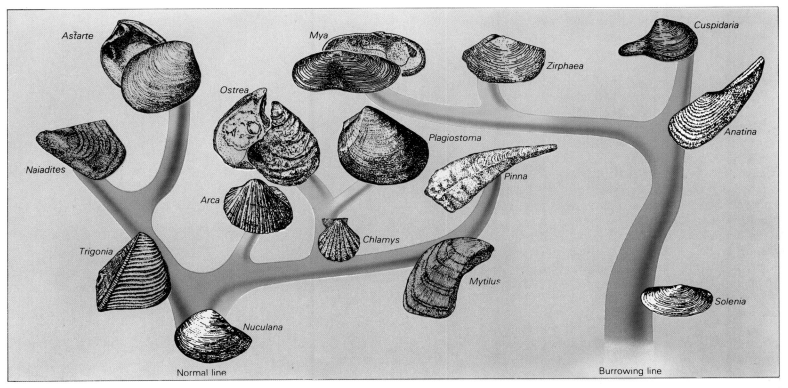

Normal line   Burrowing line

were specially modified to perform tasks to do with feeding or protection.

Bivalves

The millions of sea-shells found along the shore-line show how successful is an important class of MOLLUSCS known as the BIVALVES. These have a soft, unsegmented body protected on the outside by a mineralized shell. Oysters, mussels and clams are typical bivalves and they illustrate the variety of a group which can be traced back to the Cambrian. Some bivalve-like molluscs are found from the Lower and Middle Cambrian but the first undoubted bivalves come from the early Ordovician. By that time the group had become considerably varied and individuals were adapted to burrowing or to sediment surface-dwelling ways of life. DEPOSIT-FEEDERS living in shallow burrows were probably the ancestors of all Ordovician types of bivalves. Surface-dwelling filter-feeders developed only after the soft parts had been modified. The success of the surface-dwellers was also partly due to their developing a horny BYSSUS, by which many attached themselves to the sea-floor to make themselves more stable.

As various types adapted towards different ways of life, so their soft parts and shell changed. By the end of the Palaeozoic some bivalves had developed tube-like siphons. These allowed the animal to draw food into its shell while it stayed buried inside and protected by the sediment.

Above: This family tree of the bivalves illustrates the possible ancestry of various groupings. The branch on the *left* illustrates the probable evolutionary links between the so-called 'normal' bivalves; that on the *right* represents the evolutionary line of the burrowing types.

E **Echinoderms** are exclusively sea creatures, most having a skeleton of porous, calcareous plates. The majority have a 5-rayed or PENTAMERAL SYMMETRY. The group includes SEA URCHINS (echinoids), starfish (asterozoans), SEA CUCUMBERS (homalozoans) and SEA LILIES (crinoids). Echinoderms have tube feet that project through the skeleton and act as the animal's organs for feeding, respiration or movement.
Eocrinoids are extinct 'SEA LILIES' from the Lower Palaeozoic. Their structure is

An open sea urchin with suckered feet

primitive, and the pores for their tube feet occur on SUTURE LINES between plate rows.
Eurypterids are extinct ARTHROPODS also known as 'water scorpions'. Their closest living relatives are the king or horseshoe crabs.
Exoskeleton is the outer skeleton of various INVERTEBRATES.

F **Filter-feeders** are animals that extract their food from water currents which are usually created by movements of their own feeding organs.

G **Gastropods** are MOLLUSCS. They have a true head, an unsegmented body and a large flattened foot.
Goniatites are AMMONOIDS with angular or zig-zag SUTURE LINES. They range from the Devonian to the end of the Permian.
Graptolites are an extinct group of HEMICHORDATES. They divide into DENDROIDS and GRAPTOLOIDS, and range from the Middle Cambrian to the Permian.
Graptoloids are GRAPTOLITES with a limited number of branches and one type of THECAL CUP — the autotheca.

Siphons gave the bivalves a fresh impetus and during the Mesozoic and Cainozoic various families made use of many habitats.

Gastropods

Like bivalves, GASTROPODS are members of the mollusc family. They include snails and slugs, as well as the small PTEROPODS. Whereas bivalves have a shell in two parts, the gastropod shell is a single unit, and it is always coiled. Gastropods are the only molluscs with their body organs twisted 180° so that the gills and anus are in the mantle cavity, just behind the head. This twisting is called TORSION and it enables the gastropods to draw back into their shells. It is unlikely that the ancestors of gastropods had this twisting, or coiled shells. But without doubt they were symmetrical, and their shells may have been cap-shaped. These ideas are supported by evidence from the early Cambrian gastropods *Coreospira* and *Helcionella,* which are both coiled in a simple PLANISPIRAL manner so that the shells remain symmetrical. In time, certain families developed an asymmetrical, HELICALLY-COILED shell that made them more stable. Coiling and torsion were probably closely linked in the evolution of gastropods, and it is more than likely that they gave the group distinct advantages over other BENTHIC creatures.

From the Lower Cambrian onwards the story of the gastropods has been one of great success. By the Carboniferous they lived in many niches within sea-dwelling communities and the first snails had migrated away from salt water. Many experts think that in order to migrate, gastropods had to develop a method of fertilization inside the body, and a penis. Once they had these, the gastropods could not only move to freshwater habitats but also on to land.

From living gastropods we can establish what the primitive examples were like. For instance, a number of the ARCHAEOGASTROPODS still retain two feather-like gills. More advanced forms, such as the MESOGASTROPODS, NEOGASTROPODS and OPISTHOBRANCHS have only one gill and even that has gill filament on one side only. Early in the Mesozoic the mesogastropods gave rise to an animal that had lost its gill but had changed the surface of the mantle cavity into a lung. This was the first PULMONATE gastropod, forerunner of today's successful land-dwelling forms.

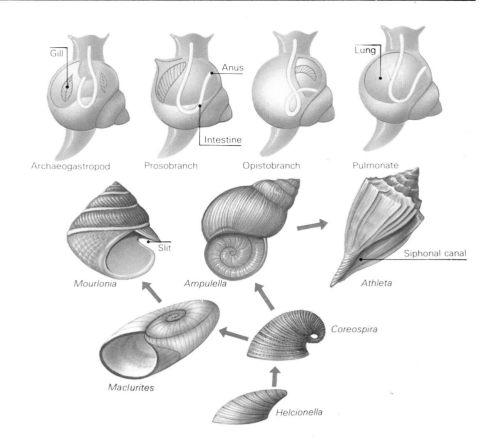

Above: The earliest ancestral gastropod probably had an uncoiled cap-like shell *(bottom).* From this arose forms which appeared flattened and were coiled symmetrically. As the gastropods became more mobile, they needed greater stability. This they achieved by developing a conical shell. The appearance of well-defined slits and siphonal canals are linked with changes in the soft parts.

Right: During their long history the gastropods have adapted to most environmental conditions. Of the 3 gastropods illustrated, *Natica* (**1**) is a marine predator which drills through the shells of its victims; *Limnaea* (**2**) is a freshwater snail; and *Helix* (**3**) is a land-dwelling snail.

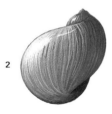

Above (top): Scientists recognize 4 major groups of gastropods, based on breathing apparatus. The 4 may represent an evolutionary sequence, with the 2-gilled archaeogastropods as the ancestors of the other groups. In turn, it is likely that the pulmonates or 'lunged-gastropods' represent the most advanced condition.

They range from the Lower Ordovician to the Devonian.

H Helically-coiled shells are found in most gastropods and some ammonites. The coils enlarge as they move down the vertical axis towards the animal's mouth.
Hemichordates are CHORDATES which lack bony tissues. They have a short rod of tissue — the notochord — above the mouth. This rod runs the entire length of the body in the higher chordates.
Hydrozoans are COELENTER-ATES which exhibit the phenomenon of 'alteration of generations'. They have an adult POLYPOID phase, and a free-swimming MEDUSOID reproductive phase.

I Inarticulates are BRACHIOPODS, most of which have skeletons with a high phosphate content. The 2 valves are unequal in size and the shell can be divided lengthwise into identical halves. No internal support structure exists for the feeding organ and the shells lack teeth for articulation.
Insects are a major group of ARTHROPODS. They are first recorded from the Devonian and today account for almost 1,000,000 species. These include the flies, beetles, lice, fleas, cockroaches, butterflies and bees. They have 6 walking legs and breathe air. Many insects have developed wings.
Invertebrates are animals without backbones.

J Jellyfish are free-swimming COELENTERATES, ranging from a few millimetres up to 2 metres across.

A king or horseshoe crab

K King crabs or horse-shoe crabs are ARTHROPODS closely related to spiders and mites. They are sea creatures with a large hinged body and spine-like tail.

L Lingula is an INARTICULATE brachiopod with a phosphatic shell. Its valves are almost identical, having BILATERAL SYMMETRY. Lingula is a burrowing animal.

M Medusoid describes the free-living, flattened phase typical of some primitive COELENTERATES, or

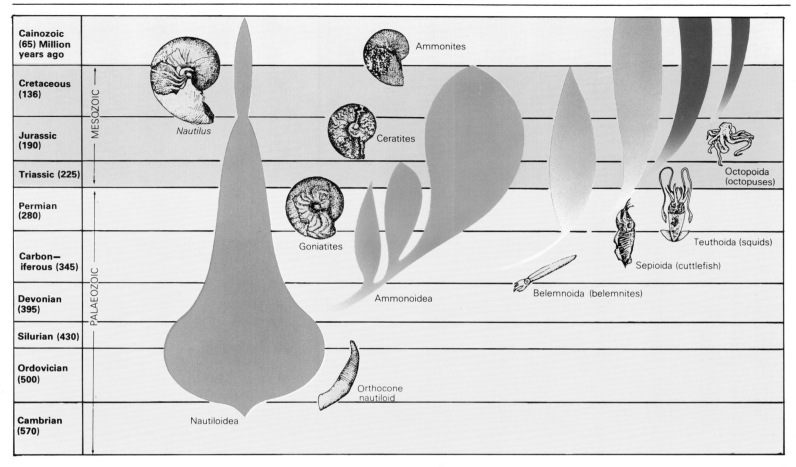

Cainozoic (65) Million years ago		
Cretaceous (136)		
Jurassic (190)	MESOZOIC	
Triassic (225)		
Permian (280)		
Carbon— iferous (345)		
Devonian (395)	PALAEOZOIC	
Silurian (430)		
Ordovician (500)		
Cambrian (570)		

Cephalopods

Like gastropods, CEPHALOPOD molluscs such as SQUIDS, OCTOPUSES and *Nautilus* have a well-defined head with well-developed sense organs. The *Nautilus* is the sole survivor of a once large and extremely varied group known as the TETRABRANCHIATA. This word implies that *Nautilus* has four gills, whereas the squids and octopuses, which are living DIBRANCHIATES, have two.

Of these groups, the tetrabranchiates have the more important fossil history, with the earliest types recorded from the Upper Cambrian. These were also the first NAUTILOIDS and their curved outer shells suggest that their ancestor was probably a single-shelled gastropod-like animal. The nautiloids flourished in the Palaeozoic and an incredible variety of shell types, often with complex inner deposits, shows that the group had fully exploited its marine habitat. By the end of the Silurian the nautiloids, or a nautiloid-

like animal, had given rise to the AMMONOIDS, which became the most successful group of cephalopods during the late Palaeozoic and Mesozoic. At first the ammonoids had rather simple SUTURE LINES. But in time these lines (which trace the junction between the inside partitions and the shell wall) became more and more complex. The trend started with the GONIATITES and continued through the CERATITES and AMMONITES. Ammonites were the peak of ammonoid evolution and their suture lines were folded into complex, rather flowery patterns.

The earliest of the dibranchiate cephalopods appeared in the Carboniferous. These belonged to the extinct squid-like BELEMNOIDS which rose to considerable importance during the Jurassic and Cretaceous. The living squids, octopuses and CUTTLEFISH probably evolved from a belemnoid ancestor some time during the Lower Cretaceous period.

Above: The family tree of the cephalopod molluscs can be traced back to the early Cambrian. The nautiloids — with simple suture lines and often with complex internal deposits — dominated the early part of the Palaeozoic era. In the Upper Palaeozoic their position was taken by the goniatites, the first of the ammonoid cephalopods. The goniatite suture line was more complex than that of the nautiloids, but simpler than that of its ceratite or ammonite cousins. Gill structure separates the nautiloids and ammonoids from the fossil belemnites, living squids and octopuses.

---

the adult JELLYFISH (medusa). **Mesogastropods** are known from the Ordovician through to the present day. They are chiefly recognized by a single large gill on the left-hand side, and by the form of the rasping tooth or radula. Living types include *Strombus* and *Nerinea*. **Metazoans** are multi-celled animals in which the cells are grouped to form tissues. This excludes SPONGES but includes COELENTERATES and all higher animals. **Molluscs** are INVERTEBRATE animals with unsegmented bodies. Although most are

sea creatures, a few, such as the snails and some bivalves, are successful in fresh water. PULMONATE snails include land-dwelling forms.

N Nautiloids were the dominant CEPHALOPODS for much of the Palaeozoic. **Neogastropods** are GASTROPODS with a single large gill on the left side. They are similar to MESOGASTROPODS but have a better developed nervous system and siphon. Neogastropods range from Cretaceous to Recent periods.

An octopus

O Octopuses are living CEPHALOPODS. They have 8 tentacles and no shell. **Opisthobranchs** are mostly 'naked', sea-living GASTROPODS such as the sea slugs and PTEROPODS. They range from the Cretaceous to Recent periods.

P Pentameral symmetry describes the distinctive 5-rayed form of many ECHINODERMS. **Periderm** is the translucent brown material that forms the skeleton of GRAPTOLITES. **Peripatus** is an ARTHROPOD with a soft thin EXOSKELETON.

It is found in tropical areas and has a muscular body, small head and numerous unjointed limbs. **Phoronid worms** are a small group of minor COELOMATE animals linked with the BRYOZOANS and BRACHIOPODS. They live on or in the sediments of the sea floor. *Phoronis* is an unsegmented animal with a horseshoe-shaped organ for feeding. **Planispiral** coiling is found in various molluscs. The shells are coiled in a single plane and appear disc-like. In most cases the shell opening and various coils can be

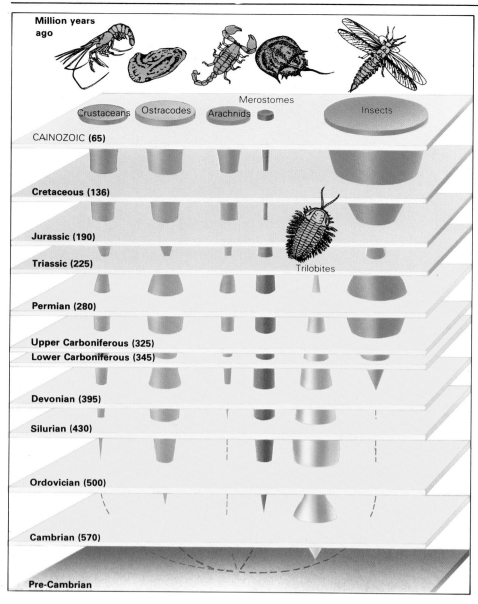

Arthropods

Of all the invertebrates the ARTHROPODS are probably the most successful and varied. They have a hard, segmented outer coat (EXOSKELETON) and limbs with joints. Living forms include the INSECTS, SPIDERS, SCORPIONS, CENTIPEDES and CRUSTACEANS. From fossils we find the extinct TRILOBITOMORPHS and the EURYPTERIDS, or giant 'water scorpions'. All these groups may possibly trace back to a common ancestor — an ANNELID WORM — but it is just as likely that several different groups of arthropods developed on their own from different forebears.

The first arthropods suddenly appear in the Lower Cambrian and from the beginning they make a strikingly varied group. This suggests that they extend far back into the Pre-Cambrian but that the first forms lacked a mineralized skeleton. In the early Cambrian there are several different classes of arthropods, with the main ones, the trilobites and trilobitoids, making up the Trilobitomorpha. The trilobitoids were the more varied of the two, but as their skeletons were very thin and lacked minerals, their fossils are confined to the fine-grained BURGESS SHALES of the Middle Cambrian of Canada. Typical trilobitoids were *Burgessia*, which looks rather like a minute KING CRAB, and *Marrella*, a rather exotic arthropod with large, backward-directed horns. Both *Marrella* and *Burgessia* have trilobite-like limbs, which had an upper gill branch and a lower walking leg. The trilobites themselves have a three-lobed exoskeleton, with a head (cephalon), body (thorax) and tail (pygidium). The earliest forms included spiny, small-tailed types such as *Olenellus* and the small, blind *Agnostus*. The fortunes of the trilobites waxed and waned during the Palaeozoic. Their general evolutionary trends were towards reducing spines, improving the structure of the eye and the appearance of larger-tailed species.

Of the other arthropod groups the first king crabs, crustaceans and onychophorans (*Aystriedia*) also appeared in the Cambrian. The king crabs are related to the giant eurypterids which range in time from the Middle Ordovician to the Permian. During the Silurian the first true scorpions appeared in land habitats, to be joined in the Devonian by mites, spiders and insects. The fossils of many non-marine groups are found only in sediments deposited under exceptional

Above: The family tree of the arthropods or 'jointed-limbed invertebrates' traces their ancestry back into the Pre-Cambrian. Little or nothing is known of their ancestors, but the group was so varied by the start of the Cambrian period, 570 million years ago, that a long period of Pre-Cambrian evolution is probable. The success of the main stocks throughout recorded time is also clearly illustrated, as is the dominance of the trilobites during the Palaeozoic era. Trilobites existed on this planet for over 340 million years, while the incredibly successful insects first appeared in the Devonian. It is likely that well over 1,000,000 species of arthropods have appeared since the dawn of the Cambrian — 900,000 species exist today. Beetles, crabs, king crabs, scorpions, butterflies, flies and lice are all examples of present-day arthropods.

---

divided equally by a horizontal line drawn across the front of the shell.

Plankton are the minute organisms that exist at and near the surface of seawater. Most of these organisms — plant and animal — float passively, but some swim in prevailing currents.

Polypoid describes the adult stage of some COELENTERATES, such as the SEA ANEMONE, and the soft parts of stony corals.

Porifera are mainly sea creatures characterized by numerous small pores and limited types of cell. Many have needle-like and branched SPICULES that may be fused to form a rigid skeleton. Among this group are the sponges, known since the late Pre-Cambrian.

Cretaceous fossil sponge

Productus is an articulate BRACHIOPOD commonly found in rocks of the Upper Palaeozoic. In most species the lower, or pedicle, valve is much the larger of the 2.

Protozoa are single-celled animals. They are mostly sea-living and their fossil record dates from the Cambrian. Several groups develop external skeletons.

Pteropods are a group of OPISTHOBRANCH GASTROPODS. They use their foot for swimming and, unlike many other opisthobranchs, often have a shell.

Pulmonates are land- or freshwater-dwelling GASTROPODS. They have lungs, not gills, and although most retain their shell, land slugs have lost theirs.

R **Radiation** is a rapid increase in the number of types in a group of organisms. It marks increased efficiency and success.

Rhabdopleura is a living HEMICHORDATE with a tube-like skeleton.

Rhynchonella is an articulate BRACHIOPOD. It has a strongly ribbed shell with a pronounced beak and poorly developed structure for its internal support.

Rugoses are a major group of 'stony corals' abundant from the Silurian to the Permian. The creatures may be solitary or live in colonies, and were important as reef builders.

S **Scleractinian** corals are solitary or colonial. They are COELENTERATES with a POLYPOID adult stage and calcareous EXOSKELETONS. They are found from the Triassic to present day.

Scorpions are close relatives of the SPIDERS and EURYPTERIDS. The earliest known

conditions, but even these 'glimpses through time' give evidence of an ever-increasing variety.

Echinoderms

Unlike most invertebrates, ECHINODERMS such as the SEA URCHINS and STARFISH have an inner skeleton made up of numerous calcite plates. These are often spiny and organized so as to give the animals five rays, or PENTAMERAL SYMMETRY. This may change to BILATERAL SYMMETRY in some sea urchins but even these remain easily recognizable as spiny-skinned animals. The echinoderms live only in the sea and their fossil record spans the last 600 million years of geological time. Little or no evidence exists, however, as to their direct ancestry, but they may have come from a worm-like organism.

The first echinoderm is probably *Tribrachidium* from the late Pre-Cambrian in Australia. Little is known of it though it is unlikely to have been the forebear of the various groups that suddenly appeared in the Lower Cambrian. These included both fixed and free-living forms. Among the creatures living fixed to the sea bottom were the first EOCRINOIDS, which looked like the living and fossil SEA LILIES (crinoids). Like the first free-living echinoderms, the eocrinoids had flexible coverings in which individual plates overlapped each other. *Helicoplacus* and *Stromatocystites* are the earliest free-living forms. Their basic design is primitive but it is difficult to place them at the foot of the evolutionary line.

Many of the Cambrian echinoderm groups lived only for a short while and this suggests that they were replaced by more efficient and better protected stocks. Rigid, stronger skeletons evolved in most groups during the Cambrian and Ordovician and examples of the living sea urchins, SEA CUCUMBERS, starfish and sea lilies had all appeared by the end of the period.

Right: The 'spiny-skinned' echinoderms are and were an extremely varied group. They are represented today by the sea urchins, starfish, sea lilies and sea cucumbers, the fossil records of which can be traced back into the Palaeozoic. Several other important groups also flourished during the Palaeozoic and one, the Carpoidea, may be linked with the evolution of the vertebrates.

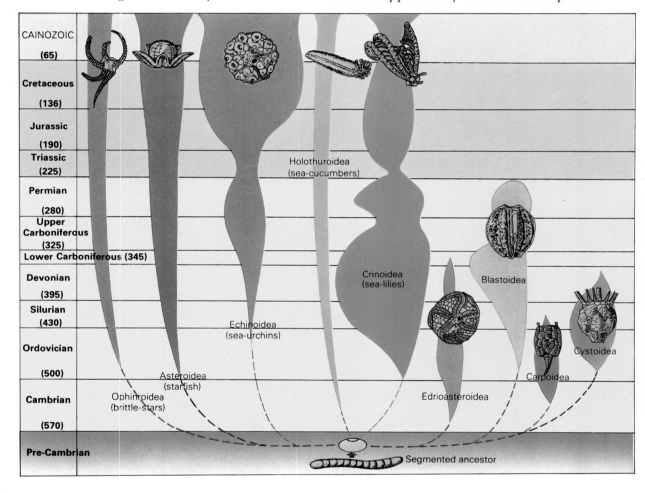

forms are from the Silurian and so they are to be regarded as the first air-breathing land-dwellers.
Sea anemones are COELENTERATES or cnidarians that lack a MEDUSOID stage in their life cycle. Their polyps are often

Fossil scorpion

large and the mouth is surrounded by a circle of retractable tentacles.
Sea cucumbers are ECHINODERMS which look rather worm-like. They lack rigid skeletons but do have calcareous SPICULES in their skin. They range from the Ordovician to the present.
Sea lilies, or crinoids, are SEA URCHINS with a cup-shaped body and single or paired arms. Primitive forms are on stalks while more advanced forms are free swimmers. Sea lilies are also known as the crinoids or feather stars, and are found

from the Lower Cambrian to Recent periods.
Sea urchins, or echinoids, are round or heart-shaped 'spiny-skins' with a rigid shell-like skeleton. The mouth is always sited on the under surface. Sea urchins are first known from the Ordovician.
Sediment surface-dwelling is a term used to describe animals or plants that live on or within the sea floor.
Spicules are needle-like or multi-rayed siliceous or calcareous structures secreted by several groups of INVERTE-

BRATES. They are most commonly associated with the SPONGES but are also found in the COELENTERATES and ARCHAEOCYATHIDS.
Spiders are ARTHROPODS with 8 legs. They belong to the arachnids and are first recorded in the Devonian.
Spirifer is an articulate brachiopod characterized by a wide hinge line and a spirally-coiled structure for internal support. Spirifers range from the Middle Ordovician to the end of the Jurassic and were most abundant during the Silurian and Devonian periods.

Sponges, see PORIFERA.
Squids are living CEPHALOPOD MOLLUSCS. They have cylinder-shaped bodies and a pen-like internal shell.
Starfish are ECHINODERMS in which the body is organized into 5 distinct rays (seldom more). They are closely related to the brittle stars but appeared several million years earlier, being recorded first in the Upper Cambrian.
Suture lines seen on the outer surface of NAUTILOID and AMMONOID shells match the contact between the internal partitions, the septa, and the shell wall.

Right: The living *Rhabdopleura* has a skeleton which is similar in structure to the extinct graptolites. *Rhabdopleura* also has a small rod of tissue above the mouth. This is the notochord found in hemichordate and chordate animals.

Zooid

Zooecium

Zooid

Rhabdopleura (Recent)

Autothecal cup

Left, right and below: Graptolites were colonial animals. Individual polyps lived in cup-like structures (thecal cups) along the edges of tubular branches (stipes).

Monograptus (Silurian)

Monograptus (Silurian)

Diplograptus (Ordovician–Silurian)

Tetragraptus (Ordovician)

Didymograptus (Ordovician)

Dichograptus (Ordovician)

Left and above: Graptolites are known to follow a number of evolutionary trends, the most important of which was probably a reduction in the number of branches. This trend began in the Cambrian period, when species with several hundred branches were common. By the Silurian single-branched forms were dominant, and each colony was characterized by fewer, larger individuals.

Dictyonema (Cambrian – Carboniferous)

Graptolites

Among the most important fossils of the Palaeozoic are the delicate, twig-like GRAPTO-LITES. Their name comes from Greek and means 'stone-writings'. It also describes the way in which they are generally preserved, for most are found as white-grey carbonized films on the surface of black shale rocks. They vary greatly in form, and colonies may range from those with a single branch to those with many. Individual branches can be straight, curved or even spiral, and the THECAL CUPS, which housed the animals, may be short or long, round, triangular or hooked. For some time graptolites were grouped with the simple HYDROZOANS, but in 1938 detailed research on their skeletons revealed that they were extinct members of the HEMICHOR-DATES, and therefore allied to the vertebrates.

Living hemichordates comprise two classes — the ACORN WORMS and the pterobranchs; and it was because the graptolite skeletons were similar to the pterobranch RHABDOPLEURA that their relationship was confirmed. The tubes of both skeletons are made from an amino-rich material (*see page 14*) known as the PERIDERM. The inner layer of this has an open mesh-work fabric and appears as a series of rings or half rings. The association of graptolites with the hemichordates suggests that they shared a common ancestor — a phoronid worm. From the late Pre-Cambrian to the Middle Cambrian the graptolite ancestors underwent several changes in their living habits. Whereas the worms lived in sediments on the sea-floor, the first graptolites were fixed sediment surface-dwellers. These belonged to the DEN-DROIDS and many were shrub-like, with numerous branches and thousands of small thecal cups. During the late Cambrian a dendroid family, the ANISOGRAPTIDAE, began to produce fewer branches and cups, and it was from this stock that the 'true' GRAPTOLOIDS arose. They flourished in the Ordovician and Silurian and followed similar evolutionary trends, with successive groups having eight, four, two and in the end, one branch. More elaborate cups was another trend and it is likely that both this and the reduced number of branches were linked to changes in feeding habits and ways of life. Unlike most dendroids the majority of graptoloids formed part of the floating, or free-swimming, PLANKTON.

Symbiosis is where 2 organisms co-exist to the benefit of each other. SEA ANEMONES and certain fish provide an example. The fish are protected by the sea anemone's poisonous tenta-

Example of symbiosis

cles and in turn clean away any waste materials.

Tabulates are an extinct group of 'stony corals'. They first appeared in the Middle Ordovician and spread rapidly throughout the world. All tabulate species lived in colonies and each individual coral was rather small. Colonies may have been loosely bound or closely packed, the individuals being polygonal in shape. Tabulates lasted until the Permian.

Terebratula is an articulate brachiopod characterized by

a smooth, tear-drop shaped shell. It has a well developed opening for the passage of its stalk (pedicle) and a loop-like structure for internal support. It spans from the Lower Devonian to Recent periods.

Tetrabranchiata are CEPH-ALOPOD MOLLUSCS with 4 gills. They are represented today by 6 species of *Nautilus*, but were once the most abundant of all molluscs. They include NAUTILOIDS and AM-MONOIDS.

Thecal cups or units occur on the outer edge of the branches of a GRAPTOLITE

colony. Each cup contained an individual animal. All the animals were linked to one another by means of a common canal.

Torsion results in the internal organs of a GASTROPOD being twisted through 180° so that the mantle cavity inside the valves faces forwards.

Trepostomes are extinct BRYOZOANS characterized by massive colonies. Each animal was housed in its own elongated and progressively thicker-walled unit. Closely spaced partitions divided each unit and the con-

struction of the skeleton earns the trepostomes the name 'stony bryozoans'. They lived from the Ordovician to the Permian.

Trilobites are extinct ARTH-ROPODS which lived only in the Palaeozoic. Their calcareous EXOSKELETON, or cuticle, divided both lengthways and sideways into 3 distinct lobes.

Trilobitomorphs are fossil sea-living ARTHROPODS. They include TRILOBITES and trilobitoids and are characterized by a limb which comprises a walking appendage and a gill branch.

The development of backbones meant that animals were able to evolve in size and
intelligence to a degree unmatched among invertebrates. Much of their success has been
due to advances in their skeletons and teeth.

Evolution of Vertebrates

The origin of animals with backbones—the
VERTEBRATES—is a subject much argued about,
especially as there is little direct evidence
provided by fossils. Fragments of the first
vertebrates come from the lowest Ordovician
rocks and although this material is less than
perfect, it shows that the vertebrates were
established by the dawn of that period. It also
shows that the search for ancestors should be
among pre-Ordovician groups. In part this is
true, but scientists must also look to the living
soft-bodied CHORDATES (*see page 26*) for vital
clues.

Forebears of the vertebrates have been sought
among many invertebrate groups, including the
worms and arthropods, but for various reasons
these have been ruled out as true contenders.
The main objections have been to their EMBRYOS,
and so attention has focused on the echinoderms.
The LARVAL stages of these 'spiny-skins' and the
acorn worms (hemichordates) are basically
similar and this may suggest that the two had a
common ancestor. Recent studies support this
view and point to the CALCICHORDATES—a group
of specialized 'echinoderms'—as the ancestors of
all the higher chordates, including the vertebrates. The evidence comes from studies of the
inner structure of Cambrian and Ordovician
calcichordates, the gills and nervous systems in
particular. Arguments for a link between the
calcichordates and vertebrates are very convincing, but many scientists still dispute it. They
prefer to link the vertebrates directly to the
TUNICATES, and believe that at some stage in the
Cambrian a tadpole-like larva of one of these
animals reproduced to give rise to a free-
swimming adult. This meant that the larva did
not develop into the normal sac-like adult living
on the sea bed, and that a different group—
similar to today's AMPHIOXUS—arose as an
ancestor to the vertebrates.

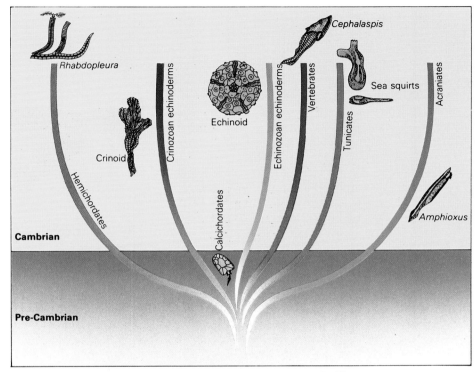

Above: The origin of
animals with backbones —
the vertebrates — is still one
of the great unsolved
problems of evolution. Of
several possible ancestors,
most cannot be counted as
direct relatives. Many
scientists believe that the
calcichordates and agnathan
(jawless) fishes, such as
Cephalaspis, are directly
linked.

Right: *Mitrocystella* is an
example of a calcichordate.
It is a flattened, rather
asymmetrical animal, with a
short tail. Recent
reconstructions of the
animal indicate that it had a
complex nervous system,
with a brain and single 'eye'.

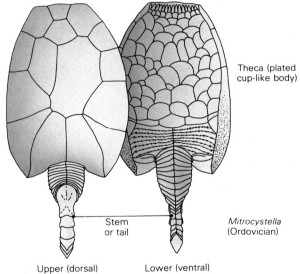

Theca (plated
cup-like body)

Stem
or tail

Mitrocystella
(Ordovician)

Upper (dorsal)　　　Lower (ventral)

Reference

A　**Acanthodians** were
the first jawed fishes.
They lived during the Silurian, Devonian, Carboniferous and Permian, and are
often called the 'spiny
sharks'. Their bodies were
covered in small, square
scales, which were crowned.
They also often had stout
spines on both lower and
upper body surfaces. The
body was streamlined and
the tail HETEROCERCAL. Few
grew more than 200 mm.

Acheulean stone tools are
commonly pointed or
almond-shaped hand-axes.
The Acheulean hand-axe
cultures take their name
from Saint-Acheul, France,
but were first developed by
HOMO ERECTUS in Africa.
Adaptive radiation occurs
when an organism or a re-
lated group of organisms
evolve into various sub-
groups which are adapted to
a wide range of ecological
NICHES (*see page 21*). For
example, there were adap-
tive radiations of fishes in
the Devonian, dinosaur-like
reptiles in the Jurassic and

flowering plants in the Cretaceous.
Aëtosaurs were primitive
THECODONTIANS, or 'tooth in
socket' reptiles. They were 4-
legged, and rather like
heavily-armoured
crocodiles. Their armour
was formed by rows of bony
plates, which in some forms,
such as *Desmatosuchus,*
were extended sideways
into large spines. The
aëtosaurs were land-
dwellers and some had pig-
like snouts, perhaps used
when rooting for food. *Desmatosuchus,* 3 metres long,
was one of the largest

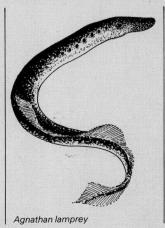

Agnathan lamprey

aëtosaurs, most of which
lived only in the Triassic.
Agnathan fishes lack jaws.
They have a sucker-like
mouth and are represented
today by the LAMPREYS and
HAG-FISHES. In the Upper
Palaeozoic, heavily ar-
moured fishes such as
Cephalaspis and *Pteraspis*
represented the agnathans.
Jawless fishes range from
the Ordovician to Recent
periods.
Amblypods are an extinct
ORDER of large UNGULATES
which lived in early Tertiary
times. They include the Pan-
todonta, such as *Corypho-*

Fish

The discovery of the fish ANATOLEPIS HEINTZI in sediments of the lowest Ordovician shows that the ancestors of the vertebrates evolved during the Cambrian. *Anatolepis* was a small jawless fish (or AGNATHAN) and it is likely that it and its close relatives were MUD-GRUBBERS, feeding on the remains of living matter. The early history of the fishes is little known until Silurian and Devonian times when the larger, heavily armoured OS-TRACODERMS flourished in sea and fresh waters. Like *Anatolepis* the ostracoderms were jawless fishes and although many later became quite active swimmers, it is hard to believe that they could have been hunters and PREDATORS. The only surviving jawless fishes are the eel-like LAMPREYS and HAG-FISHES, which lack the bony covering of their ancient relatives. The lamprey has a sucker-like mouth and unlike the armoured ostracoderms has adapted to a SEMI-PARASITIC way of life. MAYOMYZON from the Upper Carboniferous is like the living lamprey and these 'soft-bodied' fishes may show what the ancestors of the jawless fishes were like.

Fish develop jaws

The first jawed (or GNATHOSTOME) fishes appeared in the Upper Silurian, and the long lapse between the first jawless fishes and this event has been taken to show a direct ancestral link between them. This may be true but it is just as likely that the jawed fishes arose independently. The evolution of jaws was a major development for the vertebrates and it allowed the fishes to make use of new niches. The main difference between agnathans and gnathosts is that the latter have fewer GILL ARCHES and the first two gill bars are modified to form jaws. Unlike their distant cousins, the first jawed fishes had rounded rather than flattened bodies and paired fins. They swam with an eel-like movement of the body and probably looked for food near the water's surface. The first jawed fishes were the ACANTHODIANS. Many were rather like sharks although few were longer than 300 millimetres. During the Devonian the jawed fishes radiated dramatically and numerous examples of both bony and CARTILAGINOUS fishes appeared, as well as the heavily armoured PLACODERMS. It seems that the acanthodians and the bony fishes (OSTEICHTHYES) are closely related. But the ancestors of the cartilaginous fishes (chondrichthyes) and placoderms seem to be linked with a different, unknown, stock.

Bony fishes

The osteichthyes have a bony skeleton, and the early forms also have an air sac. Typical bony fishes are cod, salmon and herring, but the coelacanth and the lungfish are perhaps of even greater evolutionary importance. The first three are typical RAY-FINNED fishes, while the last two are commonly called lobed or TASSEL-FINNED. Examples of both groups first lived during the Lower Devonian. Ray-finned fishes are less advanced in evolution, even though they now have tens of thousands of species. This exceeds the number of living tassel-finned species and may show that although ray-finned fishes were more 'primitive', they were better adapted to the fast swimming, hunter-predator role.

Among the ray-finned fishes, or actinopterygians, the general trends were linked with improvements in swimming and feeding. Heavily scaled forms were gradually replaced by fishes with thin, overlapping scales and a more flexible body. Changes to the jaws and tail took place, and a swim-bladder developed, so that during

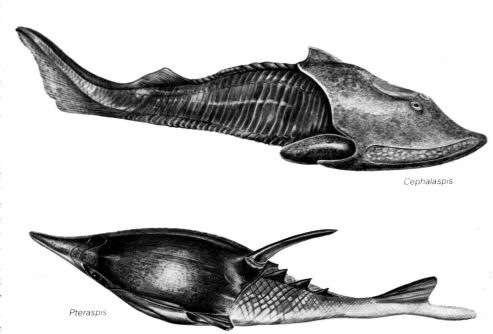

Cephalaspis

Pteraspis

Above: *Cephalaspis* and *Pteraspis* are examples of agnathan, or jawless, fishes. They represent the 2 main families of the agnathids, both of which flourished during the late Silurian to early Devonian periods. Both fishes had a thick bony armour over the outside of the body.

Below: The under-surface of the head of *Cephalaspis* is characterized by a sucker-like mouth and a circle of gill openings.

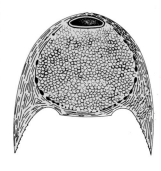

---

don, and the Dinocerata, which culminated in the grotesque *Uintatherium*.
Amia is a living example of an HOLOSTEAN fish. Its ancestry can be traced back to the Upper Palaeozoic, and it is from this type of fish that the TELEOSTS arose. *Amia* is also known as the freshwater bowfin. It has a long body and dorsal fin. The body is covered in thin scales and both lobes of the tail are about the same size.
Amniote egg is characteristic of the reptiles and birds. It has a shell for protection, a series of membranes which

allow the developing young to be bathed in fluids and a supply of nourishment (yolk). The young reptile or bird develops in a protected environment and so there is no obvious need for a larval stage as in the amphibians. The young hatchlings are small replicas of the adult.
Amphicyonidae are extinct 'bear-dogs' which lived from

Amphioxus

Oligocene until late Pliocene times. Apart from size, they had few bear-like features.
Amphioxus is a small marine animal that looks rather like a translucent fish. It is not a VERTEBRATE, but does have a well-developed NOTOCHORD, and the presence of gill slits shows that it has a distinct relationship with the vertebrates.

Anapsid describes the type of skull found in turtles and certain groups of early reptiles. The anapsid skull has no openings on the temples behind the eye.
Anatolepis heintzi is the name given to the first 'fish'. It is known from rocks of the Lower Ordovician in Spitsbergen, Norway, and is thought to be older than other remains found in the USSR and North America. No skull or fins are known, but small scales indicate the animal's link with the fishes.
Ancylopoda are an extinct sub-group of the PERISSODAC-

TYLA, consisting of the clawed CHALICOTHERES and their ancestors. They were perhaps related to the TITANOTHERES.
Ankylosaurs were a group of heavily-armoured Upper Cretaceous dinosaurs, the 'armour' being formed from large bony plates.
Anthracotheres are extinct members of the Suina, a sub-group of the ARTIODACTY-LA. They lived from Eocene until Pleistocene times, and in the late Pliocene probably gave rise to the hippopotamuses.
Anthropoids are advanced

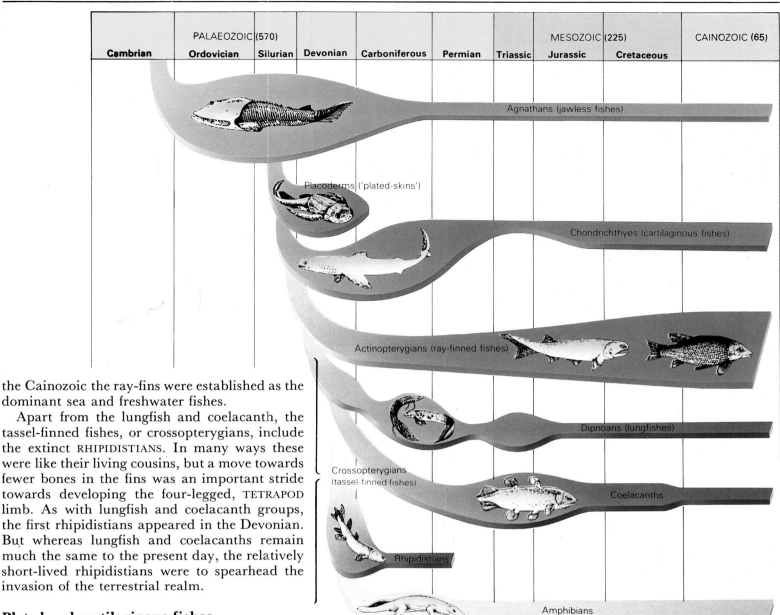

Above chart labels:

PALAEOZOIC (570)						MESOZOIC (225)			CAINOZOIC (65)
Cambrian	Ordovician	Silurian	Devonian	Carboniferous	Permian	Triassic	Jurassic	Cretaceous	

Agnathans (jawless fishes)

Placoderms ('plated-skins')

Chondrichthyes (cartilaginous fishes)

Actinopterygians (ray-finned fishes)

Dipnoans (lungfishes)

Crossopterygians (tassel-finned fishes)

Coelacanths

Rhipidistians

Amphibians

the Cainozoic the ray-fins were established as the dominant sea and freshwater fishes.

Apart from the lungfish and coelacanth, the tassel-finned fishes, or crossopterygians, include the extinct RHIPIDISTIANS. In many ways these were like their living cousins, but a move towards fewer bones in the fins was an important stride towards developing the four-legged, TETRAPOD limb. As with lungfish and coelacanth groups, the first rhipidistians appeared in the Devonian. But whereas lungfish and coelacanths remain much the same to the present day, the relatively short-lived rhipidistians were to spearhead the invasion of the terrestrial realm.

Plated and cartilaginous fishes
Of the remaining fish groups the placoderms or 'plated-skins' lived only in the Devonian (and possibly the Lower Carboniferous). There were numerous forms in both sea and freshwater niches, and a few species reached almost 9 metres in length. Unlike their close relatives the cartilaginous fish (sharks, rays and RATFISH), placoderms had heavy armour. The first sharks are known from the Middle Devonian and the first rays from the Middle Jurassic. Their early examples are similar to modern species.

Above: The first 'proto-fishes' appeared in the Cambrian period and the first jawless fish, *Anatolepis*, in the earliest Ordovician. Jawless fishes dominated the early history of the group but by the late Silurian to early Devonian, true jawed fishes were well established. The latter included the 'plated-skins', or placoderms, and cartilaginous and bony fishes. It is thought that the placoderms and cartilaginous fishes, such as the sharks and rays, are closely related and clearly separate from the ray- and tassel-finned bony fishes. Ray-finned fishes account for the vast majority of living species, but it is from the tassel-fins that the amphibians probably arose.

PRIMATES. They include the OLD WORLD MONKEYS, NEW WORLD MONKEYS, the great apes (gibbons, chimpanzees, orangutans, gorillas) and man.
Arch vertebrae are found in ancient LABYRINTHODONT amphibians. In the early development of the animal these vertebrae are formed by the hardening of several units of soft tissue.
Archaeopteryx is the first known bird. Only 5 fossils are known, 3 of which are very well preserved with excellent impressions of both tail and wing feathers. Ar-

Gibbon, an anthropoid

chaeopteryx was probably unable to fly and had a build similar to small COELUROSAURS such as *Compsognathus*.
Archosaurs are reptiles with a DIAPSID type of skull. Unlike the snakes and lizards, archosaurs keep the bony bars between the 2 temple openings. Crocodiles, dinosaurs, PTEROSAURS and THECODONTIANS are all archosaurs.
Artiodactyla are hoofed animals with an even number of toes, either 4 or 2, on each foot. They are the most numerous of the plant-eating MAMMALS.
Astrapotheres are an extinct order of large, possibly amphibious, South American UNGULATES, which lived from Eocene until Miocene

times. They may have had a proboscis or trunk.
Australopithecus was the first undoubted HOMINID to be discovered. The name means 'Southern Ape,' but we now know that *Australopithecus* belonged to the family of man. It is not clear whether the Australopithecines were ancestors of *Homo*, or true man, or whether they and *Homo* derive from a common ancestor. The latter seems more likely.

B **Baluchitherium** was one of the giant, horn-

less rhinoceroses that lived in Asia during Oligocene and Miocene times. It was the largest and heaviest land mammal ever, standing over 7 metres tall, and browsed trees, much like a giraffe.
Baptornis is a fossil seabird known from rocks of the Upper Cretaceous. It was rather grebe-like in appearance and lived at the same time as HESPERORNIS and ICHTHYORNIS. Baptornis could fly, but its wings were not as well-developed as those of the 'fish-bird' *Ichthyornis*.
Binocular vision is achieved when an animal's

Evolutionary trends among the fishes

A summary of general evolutionary trends in the various fish classes must obviously include the development of jaws and a reduction in the amount and thickness of outer armour. It may be that the true jawed fishes arose more than once from different yet related ancestors. But while this idea is a theory only, the reduction of armour is a common trend in most groups. We have seen that in ray-finned fishes the reducing of armour is linked with a general improvement in swimming power and control. This is also true of other fishes. In those of the CEPHALASPID type, the development of fins and a shortening of the head shield are related trends. Thick body scales are generally seen as primitive in most groups and among the earliest jawed fishes the short-bodied CLIMATIOIDS have thick, high crowned scales. The short body is also a primitive feature and more specialized forms, such as XYLACANTHUS, have a longer body with light armour. Another trend in the earliest jawed fishes, the acanthodians, produced the jaw structure and loss of teeth in more specialized types. Again, the reduction of armour in the acanthodians has been linked with improvements in swimming. But improvements in feeding and defence also occur.

The early bony fishes (osteichthyes) had rather simple cheek structures and the most primitive PALAEONISCID fishes had to swallow their captives whole. Later forms allowed for greater movement and better methods of feeding. These adaptations were also linked with reductions in body armour and changes in the shape of the tail. They resulted in a more efficient type of fish and one which was ideally suited to a predator's life. Among ray-finned fishes the trend was towards animals with long, streamlined bodies. But several deep-bodied forms have evolved as successful adaptations. One example, *Dorypterus* from the Upper Permian, has a flattened body 'crowned' by a long dorsal fin and a rather narrow tail. It has a small mouth and no teeth, which makes scientists believe that it fed on soft plants. Many modern deep-bodied fishes are specially adapted to living in a reef habitat.

The Palaeozoic forms of ray-finned fishes are generally grouped under the title CHONDROSTEI. They represent a primitive level of evolution and present-day examples are the freshwater POLYPTERUS and the living sturgeons such as *Acipenser*.

Above: *Anglaspis,* from the Lower Devonian. This is another example of an agnathan fish, the body of which is covered with a heavy armour of bony plates.

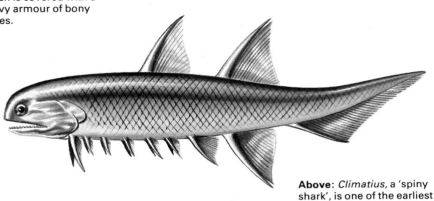

Above: *Climatius,* a 'spiny shark', is one of the earliest true jawed fishes. It has reduced external armour which is made up of small scales.

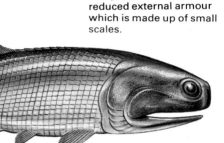

Above: *Moythomasia* is a representative of the early ray-finned bony fishes. Its body was covered by a layer of thick, overlapping scales. In later forms of such fish, these scales are often reduced, and sometimes lost altogether.

Below: *Cladoselache,* a Palaeozoic shark, had only a few scales over its body. Other Palaeozoic sharks, however, were covered in rather thick scales which seem to have thinned down to the rough skin, or shagreen, of living forms.

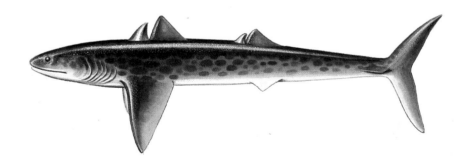

---

fields of vision overlap. Both eyes can then focus on the same object, and so estimate distance.
Bipedal animals walk on their hind legs. Many THECODONTIANS, dinosaurs and mammals — including man — are bipedal.
Bird-hipped dinosaurs, or ornithischians, are those in which the pubis bone has moved back to a position beneath the ischium bone. This results in a 3-pronged arrangement of the pelvis, similar to that found in birds. It is very different from the pelvis of LIZARD-HIPPED di-

nosaurs and other reptiles.
Bone-headed dinosaurs, or pachycephalosaurs, had a thick layer of bone over the brain case. They were bird-hipped, and seem to have lived in herds in upland regions during the Upper Cretaceous.
Borhyaena was a large, long-tailed dog- or wolf-like MARSUPIAL that inhabited South America during the Miocene.
Bovoids include the North American pronghorn (of the Antilocapridae family) and the extremely diverse range of antelopes, wild cattle,

sheep and goats (of the Bovidae family).
Brachydont teeth are short or low-crowned cheek-teeth. They are characteristic of mammals which eat a mixed diet, and of those plant-eaters which consume mainly soft leaves.
Browsers are MAMMALS which eat the shoots and leaves of trees (as opposed to grazers which eat grass and other herbs). Many dinosaurs were also browsers.
Bunodont cheek-teeth have low, rounded cusps giving them a hillock-type appearance. They are typical of

Giraffes are browsers

animals that eat a mixed diet, such as pigs and men.

C **Cainotheres** were small, rabbit-like creatures belonging to the ARTIODACTYLA. They were RUMINANTS and were restricted to Europe. After their appearance in the Eocene, they reached their heyday in the Oligocene and became extinct in Miocene times, apparently displaced by ancestors of the true rabbit.
Calcichordates are an extinct group of echinoderms which have a definite link with the CHORDATES (*see page*

Chondrostei were replaced in the Triassic by the SUBHOLOSTEANS, which have considerably thinner scales. The subholosteans were replaced in turn by the true HOLOSTEANS (Holostei) during the Jurassic. These have even thinner scales and their jaws have been greatly modified. Holosteans thrived during both the Jurassic and Cretaceous periods, but today their only examples are the garfishes and AMIA. The downfall of the holosteans was linked to success among the TELEOSTS, the most varied group of living fishes. These simply reflect the climax of trends started in the Palaeozoic: their scales are extremely thin and their tails HOMOCERCAL.

Changes in the feeding apparatus can also be seen in the evolution of the placoderms, where several levels of organization have been recorded. These are closely linked with alterations in the shape of the body, and together they reflect important changes in ways of life. At first the placoderms were slow predators living on the sea bottom, but in time fish such as *Dunkleosteus* became active in mid-waters.

The primitive level of organization in cartilaginous fishes is shown by *Cladoselache*, the earliest shark. It grew to about 2 metres in length, and is primitive because it lacked claspers, had a large keel-like pectoral (underside) fin and a symmetrical tail. More advanced sharks develop a HETEROCERCAL tail and the

Left: *Holopteryx* is a spiny-finned teleost and an ancestor of the living squirrel fishes. Teleosts are the most advanced ray-finned fishes, and the deep-bodied *Holopteryx* is but one of the great variety of forms that evolved within the group.

Right: *Caturus* is an extinct relative of the living bowfin *Amia*. Unlike *Palaeoniscum*, it has a small, rather symmetrical tail-fin and thinner scales. *Caturus* represents a more advanced level among the ray-fins than *Palaeoniscum*.

Left: *Palaeoniscum* is the genus after which the primitive ray-finned fishes — the palaeoniscids — are named. They were mostly meat-eating fish, with an elongate, streamlined body and a very unequally divided, or heterocercal, tail.

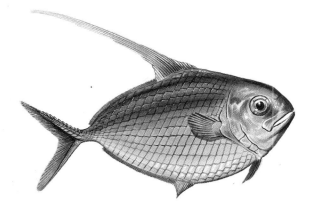

Above: *Dorypterus* is a ray-finned fish from the Upper Permian. It had a deep body and very long dorsal fin. The skull bones were small and there were no teeth. Small-mouthed, deep-bodied fishes are often found today in coral reef communities, and *Dorypterus* may have occupied a similar niche in the Permian.

organs for both feeding and movement are much changed. Most shark teeth have a high central point but during the Mesozoic some HYBODONTOID sharks developed flat teeth for crushing seashells. The fact that the cartilaginous fishes developed claspers shows that they had also developed a method of internal fertilization.

From fish to amphibian
During the Middle Devonian an important radiation took place among the bony fishes. This affected ray- and tassel-finned fishes alike and for the first time forms appeared that were able to move deliberately, albeit slowly, over land. These fishes probably lived in shallow water and in times of drought they would be forced to migrate from pond to pond. They were related to the lungfish and coelacanths and called rhipidistians. The fewer number of bones in rhipidistian

Above: Living lungfishes, such as the African *Lepidosiren*, have developed means to withstand periods of drought by making a burrow in which to retreat. But this way of adapting to seasonal aridity was of limited importance in evolutionary terms.

26). They existed during the Lower Palaeozoic, and had skeletons made up of calcite plates. Most had a large 'body' and a short tail or stem. It is thought that many lay flat on the sea-floor, using their tails as 'fixing' devices.
Canidae are the family to which the modern dogs, wolves, jackals and foxes belong. Dogs have remained less specialized than other members of the CARNIVORA, which helps explain why they are so widespread, with representatives on every continent except Antarctica.

Canines are long, cone-shaped stabbing teeth, which are especially well developed in the CARNIVORA. In sabre-tooth cats the upper canines were greatly elongated and used for stabbing and slicing.
Canoidea are a super-family of the CARNIVORA. According to a recent classification they include the AMPHICYONIDAE, CANIDAE, PROCYONIDAE, OTARIIDAE and URSIDAE. In this new scheme the MUSTELIDAE are grouped together with the PHOCIDAE into another super-family, the Musteloidea.

Carnassials are modified cheek-teeth which developed in both the CARNIV-

Walrus tusks

ORA and CREODONTS. They have a serrated cutting edge and close together like scissor blades. Carnassials are therefore adapted to slicing meat and cutting tough sinews.
Carnivora are an ORDER of mainly meat-eating MAMMALS. In older classifications, land carnivores are called fissipeds, while the sea lions, walruses and seals are called pinnipeds.
Carnivore is an animal that feeds on other animals.
Carnosaurs were the major dinosaur predators, the best-known being *Tyrannosaurus*

rex. They were LIZARD-HIPPED dinosaurs.
Cartilaginous fishes, such as the sharks and rays, do not have a bony skeleton. Instead it is made up of cartilage—a relatively soft, translucent tissue made up of rounded cells. Cartilage shrivels when the animal dies and therefore complete sharks or rays are rarely discovered in fossil form. As a result the study of these fishes is confined mostly to their teeth. The first cartilaginous fishes are known from the latter half of the Devonian. *Cladoselache*, the

Left: The skeleton of the tassel-finned fish *Eusthenopteron,* although typically fish-like in appearance, marks an important advance in the evolution of amphibians and higher land-dwelling vertebrates.

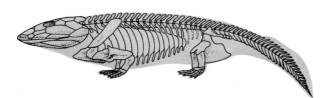

Left: The skeleton of *Ichthyostega,* the earliest amphibian, still retains a few fish characteristics, the most obvious being a bony, fin-like tail. Its short, strong limbs are a considerable advance on the tassel-fins of crossopterygian fishes.

Below: A fish has only the deep-seated apparatus of its inner ear. Without an ear drum or delicate ear bones, the fish cannot actually hear sound. Instead it picks up the vibrations from noise, and these pass along the side of the body to the brain-case. The fish ear is therefore an organ mostly used for balance and protection.

Below: In contrast to the fish ear, that of an amphibian has undergone radical changes. The ear bones are now well-developed and there is also an ear drum. Together these structures transmit vibrations to the inner ear, and hearing becomes the organ's main function, although balance is still important.

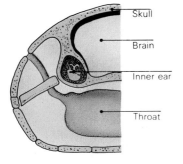

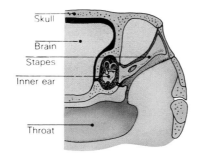

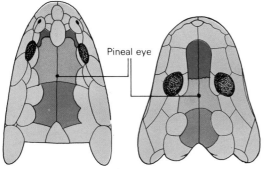

Left: A direct comparison of the skulls of *Eusthenopteron* and *Ichthyostega* shows certain similarities. Another amphibian, *Elpistostege,* appears to fall midway between, especially as regards the proportions of the skull mosaic's central bones.

fins is an obvious trend towards a four-legged creature. But other important clues to the ancestors of amphibians can be found by comparing skulls and individual teeth.

The skull roof of *Eusthenopteron,* a typical rhipidistian, is similar to that of an early amphibian. Although the *Eusthenopteron* skull has more bones, their pattern around the eye-sockets and the 'third eye' (PINEAL OPENING) is almost identical. The early amphibian's snout is longer and the area behind the eye-sockets shorter. Such changes can be expected in land-dwellers and fortunately the discovery of the 'missing link' ELPISTOSTEGE, from the Upper Devonian of Canada, proves that the changes progressed gradually. Little is known of *Elpistostege,* but the pattern of its skull bones falls between those of *Eusthenopteron* and *Ichthyostega,* the first amphibian.

Ichthyostega was a LABYRINTHODONT amphibian, a name given because their teeth appear folded, or labyrinthine, in cross section. Rhipidistians have teeth which are also labyrinthine, and such evidence obviously supports a direct descent from rhipidistian to labyrinthodont. Unfortunately not all amphibians are labyrinthodonts and it seems that a separate ancestor, or ancestors, must be found for the LEPOSPONDYLS, which are often smaller and possibly less specialized creatures.

One of the main differences between the rhipidistians and their descendants is the way in which the ear is formed. A fish ear is mainly used for balance, and its 'hearing' is limited to picking up vibrations transmitted from the body to the brain case. The inner ear is isolated. On land this would be useless, so a new device, the ear drum, was developed to pick up sound vibrations from the outside through a small, usually thin, bone called the stapes.

Relationships in the amphibian family

Remains of *Ichthyostega* have been discovered from the late Devonian sediments of east Greenland. There is no doubt that they are from a labyrinthodont amphibian, and together with *Elpistostege* and *Otocratia,* *Ichthyostega* forms the primitive Ichthyostegalia group. These animals are known only from the Upper Devonian and Lower Carboniferous and some PALAEONTOLOGISTS see them as the basic stock for both labyrinthodonts and lepospondyls. Others doubt

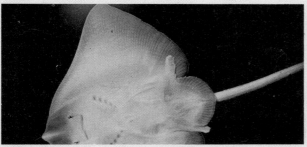

Cartilaginous fish, a ray

Devonian shark, is among the earliest cartilaginous fishes. The cartilaginous skeleton may be the primitive condition among the vertebrates, or it may be the result of young fishes reaching sexual maturity before their skeletons had turned to bone.

Cephalaspid fishes were common during the Devonian. They were jawless and had a sucker-like mouth on the under-surface of the head. The head was broad and rather flat, with two large eyes placed high on the upper surface. The tail was quite strongly developed and suggests that *Cephalaspis* was an active swimmer.

Ceratomorpha are a sub-order of the PERISSODACTYLA, and include the rhinoceroses and tapirs.

Ceratopians, or horned dinosaurs, had a large bony frill and beak-like jaws. Most of these rhinoceros-like animals had heads with a large nose-horn and 2 large, sometimes enormous, brow-horns. They lived during the Upper Cretaceous.

Chalicotheres are extinct PERISSODACTYLA, the more recent of which, such as *Moropus,* resembled clawed horses. They may have used their claws for digging up roots and tubers, or for bending down leafy branches. The group ranged from the Eocene to the Pleistocene.

Chondrostei are a group of RAY-FINNED FISHES. Today they are represented by forms such as *Polypterus,* a heavy scaled fish with lungs. Chondrostei are perhaps the most primitive ray fins, and were plentiful during the Palaeozoic and Triassic.

Climatioids were a group of 'plated-skinned' fishes — PLACODERMS. They looked more 'normal' than many of their relatives, being rather shark-like, and lived during the Upper Palaeozoic.

Coal Age is another name for the Upper Carboniferous. In North America this period

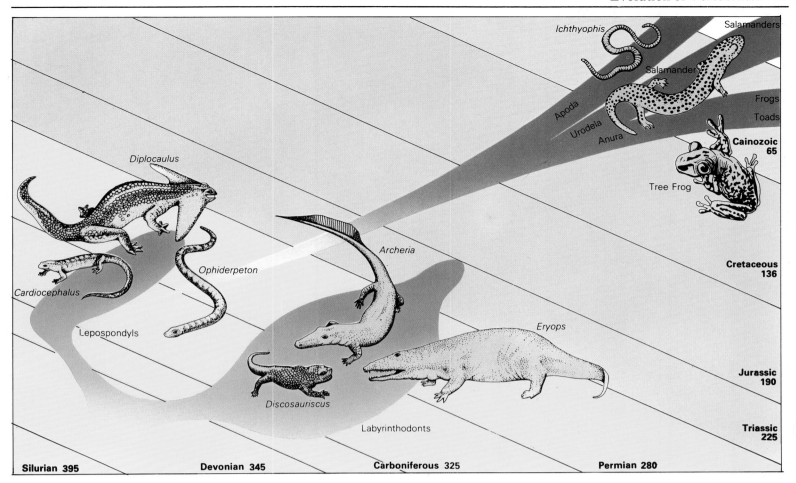

this and suggest that the two groups rose independently from the fishes. The labyrinthodont fossils are earlier, but the great variety shown by lepospondyls indicates that they too probably began during the Lower Devonian. From the Devonian to the Middle Jurassic the labyrinthodonts remained the chief amphibians, while the less important lepospondyls died out in the Permian. Some, such as SAUROPLEURA and OPHIDERPETON, were snake-like; others had small limbs and large 'horned' heads. None rivalled the labyrinthodonts in size and only a few could move beyond their ponds or lakes.

This was also true for most labyrinthodonts, for like all amphibians they had to return to water to produce young. The labyrinthodonts showed a greater variety, however, and the SEYMOURIAMORPHS especially became very well adapted to land habitats. The evolution of the labyrinthodonts involved losing the fish-like tail

of *Ichthyostega*, a general flattening of the skull and the body, and a strengthening of the limbs and shoulder and hip girdles.

During the Triassic period the first modern amphibians appeared. Between these and the ancient orders there is a considerable gap, and no groups exist to bridge it and provide any direct evidence for their ancestry. Frogs, NEWTS and SALAMANDERS show some characteristics of various ancient amphibian families, but the way their backbones are constructed suggests that a lepospondyl was their ancestor.

Types of backbone

In lepospondyls and modern amphibians the backbones, or vertebrae, have a spool-shaped body called a centrum below the NEURAL ARCH. The centrum is a single structure, pierced by a hole for the NOTOCHORD to pass through. As in the labyrinthodonts, each vertebra is very bony,

Above: The amphibian family tree clearly illustrates the 3 sub-divisions of the group. Labyrinthodonts and lepospondyls dominated the Palaeozoic era, while living frogs, toads and salamanders are important from the Jurassic onwards. The evolution of labyrinthodonts from the tassel-finned fishes is widely accepted, but the early evolution of both the lepospondyls and the recent amphibians is still a matter of discussion.

---

of time is known as the Pennsylvanian.

Coelophysis is one of the best-known COELUROSAURS. Its name means 'hollow-

Chondrosteus

form lizard'. *Coelophysis* was a small, 2-legged animal with strong hind limbs. It was a meat-eater and its long, pointed head had

numerous small, serrated teeth. Both neck and tail were long, the latter serving to balance the animal while it was running. Adults grew to 3 metres long and weighed about 20 kg. *Coelophysis* was a LIZARD-HIPPED dinosaur.

Coelurosaurs were an important group among the dinosaurs. Many were meat-eaters but others became specialized as egg-stealers and nest-robbers. All coelurosaurs were BIPEDAL and it is thought that one group, the dromaeosaurids, had comparatively large

brains as well as very good sight.

Condylarths were primitive hoofed animals which first appeared in the late Cretaceous and became extinct in the Miocene. They are ancestors of the modern hoofed animals or UNGULATES.

Convergent evolution occurs when organisms which are unrelated, except through distant ancestors, grow to look alike outwardly in the process of adapting to the same basic way of life.

Creodonts were primitive carnivorous MAMMALS. The

earliest members of the ORDER date from the late Cretaceous, and the last representatives died out in the Pliocene. In Eocene times they were the dominant mammal predators. They had relatively small brains and were therefore poorly equipped to hunt in packs or stalk the more advanced UNGULATES that began to appear in early Tertiary times.

Crocodiles and alligators are members of the ruling reptiles or ARCHOSAURS. They are closely related to the dinosaurs and pterosaurs, and like them evolved from a

as would be expected in animals where the backbone has to support the weight of the body. But the labyrinthodonts have vertebrae made up from several bony units and their relatively complex structure can be traced back to the rhipidistians. The vertebrae of lepospondyls are often called 'HUSK VERTEBRAE' while those of the labyrinthodonts and higher vertebrates are 'ARCH VERTEBRAE'. The arch type were much more flexible for possible evolutionary change, and it appears that two lines developed from the first labyrinthodonts. The main one led to the reptiles and mammals, while the second reached its peak in the advanced STEREOSPONDYLS. These large amphibians derived from the Permian genus *Eryops*. Its descendant MASTODONTO-SAURUS, the largest of all labyrinthodonts, was about 6 metres long.

Mastodontosaurus lived during the Triassic, a period which saw the labyrinthodonts rapidly decline into extinction. The chart opposite clearly illustrates this event; it also shows the times when the amphibian group undertook important radiations. The first happened during the warm, humid swampland conditions of the Upper Carboniferous, and the second during the late Cretaceous and Cainozoic. In the Carboniferous, large forms such as LOXOMMA, MEGALOCEPHALUS, *Eogyrinus* and *Diadectes* all flourished under ideal conditions. These were labyrinthodonts and they dominated both marsh and inland regions. *Eogyrinus* was adapted to water and it grew to about 5 metres long. The more heavily built *Diadectes* had strong limbs and was slightly shorter, but its reptile appearance shows a definite attempt at adapting to life on land. Both were important predators and they probably fed on smaller labyrinthodonts and lepospondyls such as *Ophiderpeton*.

Loxomma and *Megalocephalus* were also predators and they too probably lived along the edges of the Carboniferous swamps. They ranged widely throughout Europe, and related forms lived in North America. In many ways they were rather primitive and could possibly have been ancestors of the sturdily-built *Eryops* and *Cacops* which lived in the Permian and were well adapted to living on land. In this *Loxomma* and *Megalocephalus* shared something with *Diadectes*, as it was an early example of a 'truly' terrestrial, or land-living, amphibian group — the seymouriamorphs.

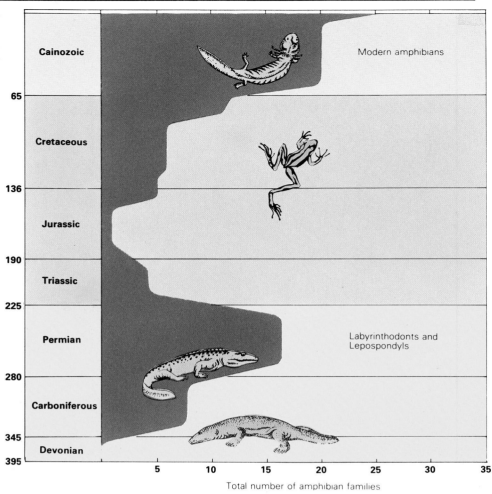

Total number of amphibian families

Left: 'Husk' vertebrae are found in lepospondyl amphibians. They are rather primitive and restricted in evolutionary potential. The centre of each unit is formed by the hardening, or turning to bone, of a single unit of cartilage.

Right: 'Arch' vertebrae are found in labyrinthodont amphibians, reptiles and mammals. 'Arch' describes the way in which the vertebra is formed by the hardening of several soft cartilaginous units.

Above: This chart illustrates the varying success of the amphibians throughout the last 395 million years of geological time. During the Palaeozoic, the labyrinthodonts and lepospondyls were extremely successful, but by the end of the Triassic they had disappeared. The Jurassic and Cretaceous represent a period of gradual expansion for the modern amphibian stocks. The number of their families now exceeds that of the labyrinthodonts and lepospondyls at their peak.

THECODONTIAN ancestor. Although the crocodiles can be regarded as primitive, they are the only archosaurs to survive the 'Age of Reptiles'. Crocodiles and alligators are 4-legged, with long snouts. They live in or along the edges of rivers or swamps, and when they move on land they have a sprawling gait. Sea-going crocodiles, such as the geosaurs, are known from the fossil record. The first crocodiles are recorded from the Triassic.

Deinotheres were hoe-tuskers, so-called be-cause they had powerful down-turned tusks on the lower jaws, which were presumably used for digging. They remained more or less unaltered throughout their existence, spanning the Miocene, Pliocene and much of the Pleistocene. One early palaeontologist thought that the *deinotheres* lived in rivers, and that at night they slept in the water, anchored to the bank with their tusks! **Desmostylids** were large mammals that lived in the shallow waters off the shores of the northern Pacific Ocean from the late Oligocene to the Middle Pliocene. Although described as a kind of 'marine hippopotamus', their skulls were more like those of primitive elephants, while other features resemble the sea cows.

Sketch of a deinotheres

Diapsid describes the type of skull in the THECODONTIANS, dinosaurs, PTEROSAURS and crocodiles. The skull has 2 openings on the temple, behind the eye. Snakes and lizards also have a diapsid skull but unlike the AR-CHOSAURS tend not to keep the bony bars between the 2 openings.
Diatrymiformes were a group of gigantic birds that existed during the Palaeocene and Eocene. They were flightless predators with huge heads and very strong legs.
Dimorphodon is a primitive

Eryops (Permian)

Ophiderpeton (Upper Carboniferous)

Diadectes (Early Permian)

Triadobatrachus (Triassic)

Ancestors of modern amphibians

The second peak in the evolution of amphibians is connected to the rise of modern groups and appearance of new varieties. This began in the early Jurassic and the number of different types which arose almost equalled the great radiation of the Upper Carboniferous. By the dawn of the Jurassic period frogs were firmly established and it seems that they can be linked back to the frog-like *Triadobatrachus* of the Triassic. This creature had a broad and flattened skull, and reconstructions show that the basic design for modern frogs and toads was set down over 200 million years ago. *Triadobatrachus* was rather short in the lower leg, however, and appears to have been more suited to crawling than leaping. Longer legged, true frogs appeared in the Lower Jurassic and by the early Cretaceous examples of most modern families existed in various parts of the world. These included the PIPIDS and LEIOPELMATIDS,

both generally seen as being primitive forms.

Of other modern amphibians, the first salamanders and newts appeared during the Upper Jurassic. Unfortunately the fossils of this group are few and only a limited number of genera are known from the Cretaceous. But it seems that like many lepospondyls, numerous early salamanders reduced the size of their limbs and became fully adapted to living in water. This is true of certain living species and the trend to smaller limbs is usually connected with the body organ of respiration becoming longer. Other salamanders live mainly on land, often being adapted to life in upland areas.

The first reptiles

Most people accept that changes in the environment are important to evolution. The same is true for competition, and together they encourage the SURVIVAL OF THE FITTEST. By this we

Above: The illustrations of *Eryops, Diadectes, Ophiderpeton* and *Triadobatrachus* provide us with a useful insight into the variety of amphibians that has existed since the appearance of the first amphibian, *Ichthyostega,* during the Upper Devonian. *Eryops* and *Diadectes* are labyrinthodonts. *Ophiderpeton* is a lepospondyl and *Triadobatrachus* is a member of the Lissamphibia. Its general appearance shows that *Triadobatrachus* is an ancestor of the living frogs and toads. Of the animals shown, *Ophiderpeton* was probably the most specialized. It had no limbs and was specifically adapted to a life in water.

PTEROSAUR recorded from Lower Jurassic rocks in Europe. It is relatively small, with a skull about 200 mm long. It had strong teeth, a long reptilian tail, and was closely related to *Rhamphorhynchus*.
Dinosauria was the name given by Sir Richard Owen in 1841 to a group of gigantic terrestrial reptiles. The name means 'terrible lizards', from the Greek *Deinos* — terrible, and *saurus* — lizard. Unfortunately the dinosaurs are not lizards and we know that their closest living relatives are the crocodiles and al-

ligators. Palaeontologists now divide the dinosauria into 2 groups — the ornithischians (BIRD-HIPPED) and saurischians (LIZARD-HIPPED). **Docodonts** are known only from fossil teeth in North American sediments of Upper Jurassic age. They were very small primitive mammals.
Domesticated animals are kept by man as sources of food and raw materials, as beasts of burden, and as pets. Selective breeding, aimed at producing various desirable features, has greatly changed domesti-

cated animals, so that often they look very different from their wild ancestors.
Dryopithecines were the earliest undoubted apes. They lived in Africa, Asia and Europe in Miocene times and looked something like chimpanzees. Almost certainly they were the ancestors of modern apes, and diverged from the same stock as RAMAPITHECUS about 15 million years ago. Since *Ramapithecus* is a forebear of man, it follows that the apes and man have developed along different lines from the outset.

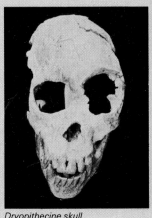

Dryopithecine skull

E **Ecological niches** are identified by the organisms inhabiting them. They may be broad enough to cover all the animals living off an area of grassland — a grazing 'niche' — or narrow enough to include the creatures living in an animal's fur.
Elpistostege is a LABYRINTHODONT amphibian known only through the incomplete skull of one small individual. But this skull is important, as the arrangement of bones on its roof seems to be at an intermediate stage between that found in the TASSEL-

Left: Skeletons of the oldest known reptile, *Hylonomus*, are found in lower sediments of the Upper Carboniferous (Pennsylvanian) in Nova Scotia, Canada. The animal probably measured a little over 200 mm, and this small size suggests that it was an insect-eater. *Hylonomus* is found in fossil tree trunks, which were probably also the habitat of its amphibian ancestors. The structure of its skeleton, particularly that of its skull, tells us that *Hylonomus* belongs to the reptiles. *Hylonomus* is the earliest of the stem reptiles, or cotylosaurs, a group which is represented today by the turtles, tortoises and terrapins.

Below: The amniote egg is protected by an outer shell. It also has its own food reserve—the yolk—and an egg 'white', or albumen, to provide the water essential to growth. These various layers are surrounded by thin membranes which enable the reptile embryo to perform all the functions essential to its development. The amniote egg was a necessary stage in adapting to life on land.

Below: Young turtles hatching from their eggs are exact replicas of their parents. They emerge after a period of incubation during which they develop within the egg, nourished by its own valuable food supply. The eggs of the turtle, known as amniote eggs, are like those of other reptiles and the birds. Developing this type of egg allowed the tetrapods to reproduce out of water. Amniote eggs are known from fossils, and those of the dinosaurs are frequently found in nests. Most reptiles do not protect their nests, but we have evidence that certain dinosaurs cared for their young, as does the Nile crocodile today. During the incubation period the parent crocodile is known to remain close to the nest. When this is over, it will carefully remove the newly-hatched young to a safer site.

mean that some animals are better adapted than others to cope with changing conditions and then to make use of them. We have already seen how rhipidistians and amphibians appeared during the Devonian, in response to strong competition and changes in climate. A similar story unfolds during the Carboniferous, but in this case the animals in question were the first REPTILES. The swamplands of the 'COAL AGE' were ideally suited to the development of amphibians, and huge animals such as *Loxomma* and *Eogyrinus* dominated. Competition for food and territory was intense, so that smaller amphibians were forced to seek shelter and food in trees and drier areas. Many began eating insects and in time they relied less on water for protection. Their bodies changed and formed a scaly skin to help prevent them from drying up. As fertilization could take place inside the body, they were able to remain on land during reproduction and, finally, developing a membrane or shell around their eggs freed them from having to find a suitable pond in which to spawn.

It is almost impossible to answer the question: which came first, the reptile or the egg? For remains of both scaly skin and the reptilian type of egg (AMNIOTE) rarely occur in the fossil record. The first reptiles are identified by the structure of their skeleton, as important characters dividing reptile from amphibian include fewer bones in the reptile skull roof, and modifications to the limbs, shoulder and hip bones. The earliest reptiles have been found in Middle Carboniferous sediments of Nova Scotia. They include the small lizard-like *Hylonomus*, remains of which were discovered inside fossilized tree trunks.

Hylonomus is found associated with other reptiles, and together they represent two distinct lines of evolution. This suggests that the split from a common ancestor had taken place during the Lower Carboniferous. *Hylonomus* is an early STEM REPTILE, or ANAPSID, having a skull in which the bony cover is pierced only by holes for the eyes and nostrils. Some of its contemporaries, however, had an extra opening on either temple, just behind the eyes. These were the first of the SYNAPSID reptiles, which ultimately gave rise to the mammals. But synapsids are advanced reptiles, and it is to *Hylonomus* and related forms that we must look for probable links with an amphibian ancestor. As a primitive reptile

Amniote egg

Shell
Albumen
Amnion
Allantois
Yolk
Chorion

Developing young reptile

FINNED fishes and that of the first amphibians.
Embrithopods are an extinct ORDER of sub-UNGULATES, from the Lower Oligocene of Egypt. The only known representative is *Arsinoitherium*, a rhinoceros-sized creature which had 2 great nasal horns arranged side by side.
Embryo is a young animal which develops in an egg shell or inside the womb of its mother. An embryo developing inside a shell obtains nutriment from the yolk. Within the womb of a mammal, the developing

embryo is supplied with nutrients through the direct umbilical link it has with its mother.
Entelodonts are extinct ARTIODACTYLA that resembled wild boars, and lived from late Eocene to Miocene times. The largest were as big as bison, which explains the description 'giant pigs'. They probably became extinct in competition with the more intelligent pigs and peccaries.
Eohippus means 'dawn horse', and is a common name for the earliest ancestor of the horse, which was

about the size of a fox-terrier. But the correct name is *Hyracotherium*, for when the first fossils of this early Eocene animal were found in Europe, they were mistakenly linked with the small African hyraxes or dassies.
Epoch is a sub-division of geological time. For example, the Oligocene and Miocene epochs are subdivisions of the Cainozoic era. An epoch is not limited to millions of years, but corresponds to a rock series, the top and bottom of which are often identified by certain fossils.

Euryapsid describes the skull type found in the PLESIOSAURS and NOTHOSAURS. Like the SYNAPSIDS, euryapsid reptiles have a single opening on the temple behind the eye socket. The opening was smaller and higher on the

Hyracotherium

Hylonomus would have kept some amphibian characters, so its solid skull roof and lack of an OTIC NOTCH are vital clues. Several groups of early four-legged animals have an otic notch, which may have marked the position of the ear drum.

In search of an ancestor

The change from amphibian to reptile is a fascinating step in the evolution of the vertebrates. Palaeontologists have searched for years among several groups of amphibians to find forms which link the two. For a long time the land-dwelling seymouriamorphs of the Upper Palaeozoic appeared to be the 'missing link'. They combined both reptilian and amphibian characters and so have been classed with both groups. Their skull roof is identical to that of some labyrinthodonts but they also have a large otic notch, which is not typical of amphibians. Modified limbs, shoulder and hip girdles also draw the seymouriamorphs closer to the reptiles, and some palaeontologists still argue that they are indeed proto-reptiles. But the discovery of large tadpole-like creatures in sediments containing SEYMOURIA suggest that it was truly an amphibian. If this is so, then the otic notch and modified limbs show that *Seymouria* and its relatives were highly specialized. As they also appear later in the geological record than the first reptiles it is unlikely that *Hylonomus* developed from such a specialized amphibian stock.

Seymouria

Above: The Permian amphibian *Seymouria* in many ways resembled a land-dwelling reptile, but it also retained some truly amphibian characters.

Right: *Seymouria's* skull was similar to that of most labyrinthodonts, but the large otic notch is like that found in some early reptiles. It was once thought that *Seymouria* was an ancestor of the early reptiles such as *Hylonomus,* but the otic notch eliminates it from this role.

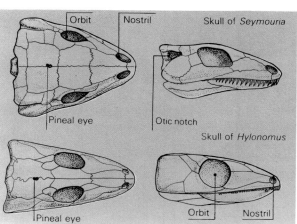

Left: The scaly skin of the reptiles helped them in their conquest of the land. Its presence was almost as important in this respect as that of the amniote egg. Scales prevented the first reptiles from drying out, and allowed them to move away from the confines of a damp environment. Scales may be thickened to provide protection against hunters, and raised to allow the animal to lose heat when necessary.

---

temple in euryapsids than in synapsids.

F **Felidae** is the family to which the cats belong. Cats appeared in late Eocene times, and diversified greatly in the Oligocene.
Feloidea are a super-family of the CARNIVORA and include the Old World civets, hyaenas and cats.

G **Genetic conservation** involves preserving the GENE (*see page 13*) 'pools' of wild plants and animals and older types of domesticated plants and animals. Their

genes could one day be used to improve existing strains of domesticated organisms, by cross-breeding, and there is potential for domesticating yet more plants and animals in the future. If they become extinct, however, none of this will be possible.
Gigantism describes the growth to a huge size by various, often short-lived, species.
Gill arches are well developed in most fishes. They lie behind the jaws and their bony elements help support both the jaws and gill apparatus.

Glacials occurred during the Pleistocene, when ice-

Hyaena

sheets covered much of the continental landmasses in the northern hemisphere. On average the larger ice-sheets were roughly 2 km thick. Altogether there have been some 17 glacials, separated by warmer INTER-GLACIALS, since the Pleistocene began about 1.6 million years ago.
Gnathostome fishes include the bony fishes, the sharks and rays, and many ancient stocks. All have jaws and are therefore easily distinguished from the AGNATHANS.
Gomphotheres were long-

jawed mastodonts from which the true elephants developed, possibly as early as the end of the Miocene. The mastodonts differed from elephants in that the crowns of their cheek-teeth had simple rounded cusps, hence the name mastodont (tooth resembling the female breast).

H **Hag-fishes** are, like LAMPREYS, living jawless fishes or AGNATHANS. They feed on dead or dying fishes. The slime hag is a typical representative of this group.
Herbivores are animals that

The search for a reptile ancestor must then concentrate on other amphibians, and as both early labyrinthodonts and lepospondyls lack an otic notch, several families can be considered.

Stem reptiles

As an anapsid reptile, *Hylonomus* was the forerunner of the living turtles, tortoises and terrapins. It was also the ancestor of a more varied group of reptiles that flourished during the Permian and early Triassic. These animals are known as the stem reptiles or cotylosaurs. Many were large, cumbersome creatures, but others were comparatively small and quite agile. Among the best-known of the earliest stem reptiles is *Limnoscelis*, a medium-sized flesh-eater from the Lower Permian of North America. It was heavily built, with a long tail and rather short legs like those of an amphibian. The head was long in the snout and the front teeth sharp and rather tusk-like — ideal for gripping and stabbing prey. *Limnoscelis* probably lived in and around swamp areas, was probably SEMI-AQUATIC and fed on the fish-eating amphibians still common in the early Permian.

A close relative of *Limnoscelis* was the more specialized stem reptile *Labidosaurus*. This small creature was about 650 millimetres long, with a comparatively large head and shortened tail. It was more graceful than *Limnoscelis* and seemingly better suited to life on land. *Limnoscelis* and *Labidosaurus* were short-lived, however, and by the mid-Permian had been replaced by a reptile group known as the PROCOLOPHONIDS. These were still stem reptiles but generally had shorter jaws and better jaw movement. Early examples were less than 350 millimetres long, but with *Pareiasaurus* and SCUTOSAURUS, which appeared during the Upper Permian, came the largest of all stem reptiles. *Pareiasaurus* and its relatives were HERBIVORES, and therefore heavily built. Weight was a problem, and changes to their limbs meant that these animals supported their bodies in a more upright fashion. Their feet were also broader and perhaps they lived 'hippo-style' along the edges of swamps. *Scutosaurus* had a rather grotesque skull, with bony protuberances giving it a fearsome appearance. But this large lumbering creature was perfectly harmless. By the end of the Permian *Pareiasaurus* and its relatives had vanished, for only a few pro-

Right: *Limnoscelis* (**1**) and *Pareiasaurus* (**2**) are examples of the stem reptiles, or cotylosaurs. They are noted for their anapsid skull, similar to that of the turtles and tortoises. *Pareiasaurus* was much the larger of the two, and rather grotesque in form. It was a semi-aquatic herbivore, whereas *Limnoscelis* was a flesh-eater. The stem reptiles flourished during the Permian. It is obvious that these rather primitive, cumbersome creatures failed to compete with their more advanced synapsid cousins, the pelycosaurs.

colophonids persisted into the Triassic — a period that belonged to the more advanced descendants of the first stem reptiles.

Most people accept that the anapsid type of skull, found in *Hylonomus* and living turtles, shows the primitive state in the evolution of the reptiles. It has no holes in the temple and the skull roof's bony shield provides more than enough protection. It is also heavy and gives only limited room for the development of important muscles. Skull types that evolved from this primitive state developed openings on the temple, making them lighter. These appeared first in the synapsid reptiles of the mid-Carboniferous, as a single opening placed low behind the eye. The later EURYAPSIDS had openings higher on the temple — such skulls are characteristic of the PLESIOSAURS and ICHTHYOSAURS. Both synapsid and euryapsid skulls are marked improvements on the anapsid type, but the most advanced design is found only in the 'ruling reptiles', the ARCHOSAURS. These include the dinosaurs and CROCODILES, the skulls of which have two temple openings and are called DIAPSID. Such holes in the skull allowed new muscles to develop, and feeding to improve.

---

eat plants as their sole source of food.
Hesperornis, the 'dawn bird', is, after *Archaeopteryx*, one of the earliest recorded birds. Its remains are known from Cretaceous rocks, and from these it is possible to determine that *Hesperornis* was a sea bird. It was quite large, the skull measuring about 250 mm in length. Both upper and lower jaws had teeth, although a horny sheath over the front of the upper beak is similar to that found in more advanced birds. *Hesperornis* had very small wings and

breastplate, and was probably a water-loving diver.
Heterocercal tail is the type commonly found in sharks. It is noted for the upturning of the lower end of the backbone and the specialized major area of fin below and behind this region of the vertebral column.
Heterodontosaurus, or the 'different-toothed lizard', lived in southern Africa during the latter half of the Triassic. It was a fast-running biped. *Heterodontosaurus* was a BIRD-HIPPED dinosaur, noted for its differ-

ent types of teeth. In many ways its dentition was similar to that of a mammal with large, tusk-like canines, and *Heterodontosaurus* prob-

A heterocercal tail

ably used its tusks during territorial battles. It had muscular jaw pouches, probably used to pass plant material across the mouth during chewing.
Hipparion was a type of lightly-built horse that lived from Upper Miocene to late Pleistocene times.
Hippomorpha are a sub-ORDER of the PERISSODACTYLA. They include the horse and the extinct TITANOTHERES and palaeotheres. The latter appeared in the Eocene and died out during the Oligocene. *Palaeotherium*, for example, was the size of

a small rhinoceros and its skull was tapir-like. This animal may also have had a short trunk.
Holosteans are bony fishes represented today by the freshwater dogfish *Amia* and the garpike *Lepisosteus*. They are characterized by their scales and by the reduced number of bones in their fins. The holosteans first appeared in the Triassic, and forms such as *Lepidotes* were plentiful during the Jurassic and Cretaceous.
Hominid is a member of the family to which man belongs.

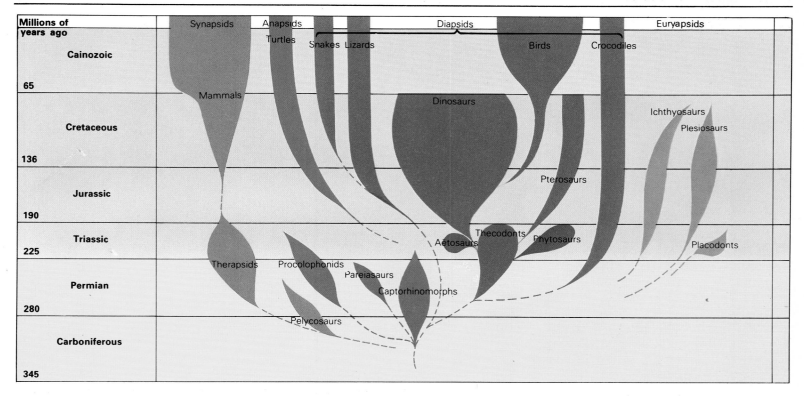

Millions of years ago		Synapsids	Anapsids		Diapsids			Euryapsids	
			Turtles	Snakes Lizards		Birds	Crocodiles		
Cainozoic									
65		Mammals			Dinosaurs			Ichthyosaurs	
Cretaceous								Plesiosaurs	
136									
Jurassic						Pterosaurs			
190									
Triassic					Aëtosaurs	Thecodonts Phytosaurs		Placodonts	
225		Therapsids	Procolophonids	Pareiasaurs					
Permian				Captorhinomorphs					
280		Pelycosaurs							
Carboniferous									
345									

In anapsid reptiles such as the marsh turtles and land tortoises, improvements in feeding and increases in the size of the jaw muscles were made possible by the gradual erosion of the rear section of the skull roof. The turtles (or testudines) as a group have no teeth, and the front part of their jaw is covered by a horny beak or sheath. The bony shell developed by turtles and tortoises is an ideal protection against predators, and though it is often thought that these anapsids have shown few advances in evolution since the Triassic, it is noteworthy that hundreds of species today occupy many niches on land and in aquatic environments. Many testudines are herbivores, but others, like terrapins and some marine turtles, are meat-eaters. Throughout the last 100 million years, several families of huge marine turtles have lived in the oceans of our planet. In the Cretaceous the gigantic *Archelon* reached almost 4 metres, and was only slightly larger than later Cainozoic forms. Today, the leathery turtle is the largest sea-dwelling reptile. Large tortoises are known from several islands, and some individual animals have been known to survive for hundreds of years.

Above: The family tree of the reptiles traces the fortunes and relationships of these advanced tetrapods over the last 300 million years of geological time. The obvious success story is that of the diapsid reptiles. Within this group we find the thecodontians, dinosaurs, crocodiles and pterosaurs.

Right: Among the reptiles, zoologists and palaeontologists can recognize 4 basic types of skull. These are identified by the presence or absence of various openings on the temple, and by the pattern of the bones behind the eye. Of the 4 types the anapsid skull, without any openings, is considered the most primitive, and the diapsid type, with 2 openings, the most advanced. The synapsid skull is typical of the mammal-like reptiles and mammals, and the euryapsid is typical of the aquatic plesiosaurs and ichthyosaurs. Both of these skull types have a single temple opening.

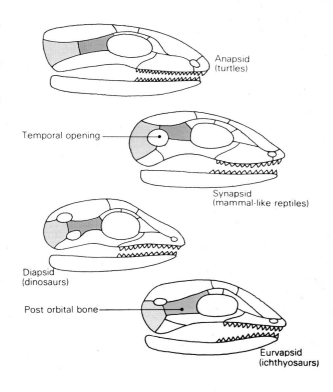

Anapsid (turtles)

Temporal opening

Synapsid (mammal-like reptiles)

Diapsid (dinosaurs)

Post orbital bone

Eurvapsid (ichthyosaurs)

Hominoid is a member of the super-family which includes the families of gibbons and siamangs (Hylobatidae), great apes (Pongidae) and that of man (Hominidae).

Homocercal tail is one in which both the fin parts are about the same size.

Homo erectus was in many ways the first 'true' man. He appeared in Africa about 1.5 million years ago and then spread to Asia before becoming extinct about 1 million years later.

Homo habilis was an early member of the group to which modern man belongs. *Homo habilis* seems to have been an ancestor of *Homo erectus,* and lived in East Africa about 1.75 million years ago. In the early 1970s, even older fossils of *Homo* were found in East Africa,

probably about 3 million years old.

Homo sapiens, or modern man, probably developed from HOMO ERECTUS somewhere between 500,000 and 100,000 years ago. Our subspecies, *Homo sapiens sapiens,* lived in Africa and Eurasia 40,000 years ago and spread to North America and Australia soon after.

Husk vertebrae are characteristic of LEPOSPONDYL amphibians. The centrum or central unit of each vertebra (backbone) is a single unit of bone pierced by a hole for the NOTOCHORD.

Hyaenidae or hyaenas are a family of the CARNIVORA, and although closely related to cats, they look very like dogs. Fossil hyaenas very similar to modern forms lived in early Pliocene times, soon after these animals first appeared in the late Miocene.

Hyaenodonts are a family of the extinct CREODONTS. Their skull and tooth row tended to be more elongated than those of the closely related OXYAENIDS.

Hybodontoids were a more progressive group of sharks that replaced the

Amia, freshwater dogfish, is an holostean

Nothosaur

Left: Small to medium-sized aquatic reptiles, such as *Ceresiosaurus* and *Nothosaurus,* were common during the Triassic. They belonged to the nothosaurs and were rather like the plesiosaurs in their overall shape.

Marine reptiles

Reptiles first appeared in water as anapsid MESOSAURS during the Upper Carboniferous. These were rather tiny animals, apparently adapted to eating crustaceans. However, they were short-lived, and not until the Middle Triassic did large numbers of aquatic reptiles appear. These included the NOTHOSAURS, PLACODONTS, plesiosaurs and ichthyosaurs.

Of these groups the nothosaurs were the least specialized and it seems that their ancestors came from land-based reptiles. The same is true for the placodonts, although these were much more specialized than the nothosaurs. Placodonts reached their peak in PLACOCHELYS, a turtle-like creature with a toothless beak, paddles and a bony shield. Both the placodonts and nothosaurs were short-lived groups, neither challenging as major marine predators. This role was shared by plesiosaurs and ichthyosaurs and, in the Upper Cretaceous, by MOSASAURS.

Plesiosaurs possibly came from the nothosaurs, but unlike their ancestors they grew to an enormous size and developed powerful turtle-like paddles. The ancestry of ichthyosaurs is unknown, but from the outset these fish-like reptiles were masters of the Mesozoic seas. Committed to an aquatic life, they were the only marine reptiles to produce live young.

Today the only successful marine reptiles are the turtles, the ancestors of which appeared during the Upper Triassic. MARINE TURTLES themselves first appeared in the Cretaceous.

Mammal-like reptiles

We saw in looking at the evolution of the earliest reptiles (*see page 42*) that anapsid and synapsid

Below: During the Mesozoic era many reptile groups other than the nothosaurs and placodonts adapted to an aquatic life. Some, like the mixosaurs and ichthyosaurs, were truly fish-like in character, while others retained a more reptilian appearance and returned to land to lay their eggs. Those which laid eggs on land included the plesiosaurs, turtles and mosasaurs. In contrast, the ichthyosaurs gave birth to live young, and can be described as viviparous. Of the animals illustrated, *Ichthyosaurus* and *Placodus* are known to have the euryapsid type of skull, and *Metriorhynchus* shows extreme adaptation to a sea-going life. Aquatic reptiles ruled the seas for over 130 million years, and mammals such as whales and dolphins did not appear until long after their extinction.

Ichthyosaurus
Placodus
Metriorhynchus

Cladoselache type of fish during the late Palaeozoic. They came between the primitive cladoselachians and modern sharks and were common during the late Palaeozoic and Mesozoic.
Hypsodont teeth are highly specialized cheek-teeth, adapted for living off a grass diet. These kind of teeth are found in the more advanced ARTIODACTYLA, PERISSODACTYLA and PROBOSCIDEANS.

I **Ice Age** is the name commonly given to the Pleis-

tocene epoch — which began about 1.6 million years ago — and during which there were repeated GLACIALS and inter-glacials. We now know that glaciation happened before the beginning of the Pleistocene and that the present Holocene epoch is also a typical inter-glacial.
Ichthyornis, the 'fish-bird', is well known from the Upper Cretaceous, and in

Ichthyosaur skeleton

particular the chalk deposits of Kansas, USA. It flew strongly and looked rather like modern seagulls or terns. *Ichthyornis* was quite small, reaching about 200 mm high. Like *Archaeopteryx*, it seems to have had teeth.
Ichthyosaur was the most highly adapted of all water-living reptiles. Ichthyosaurs lived through most of the Mesozoic, but were especially common in the Jurassic. They were already highly specialized for living in water when they first appear in Triassic rocks. But no

earlier forms are known.
Incisors are nipping teeth, though some may be developed into a chisel-type shape — as in the rodents — while in elephants they have become tusks.
Insectivorous animals live on an insect diet.
Inter-glacials, see GLACIALS and ICE AGE.

K **Kuhneosaurs** were a group of ancestral lizards that had a pair of horizontal 'sails' or 'wings'. They were among the first reptiles able to glide and lived during the Triassic.

types appeared at the same time. The anapsids were primitive, while the earliest synapsids can be seen as the basis for one of the greatest evolutionary stories of all. Its probable end is with the development of man, but farther back in time it includes chapters on the evolution of the PELYCOSAURS and the mammal-like THERAPSIDS.

The first synapsids were much the same as their contemporaries, with few of the modifications in teeth and skull shown in later groups. Pelycosaurs such as *Dimetrodon* and *Edaphosaurus* are examples of the next stage in synapsid evolution. The large 'sails' on their backs were probably an attempt to regulate the temperature of their bodies. *Dimetrodon* also showed important developments in its teeth — some resembled the incisors, canines and cheek teeth of the later therapsids and mammals. Specialization of different teeth was a major evolutionary advance, enabling an animal to break its food down into smaller pieces. These could be more readily digested, allowing the creature to gain the energy it needed much more rapidly. In time some pelycosaurs were able to control the rate at which they burned their food to produce heat and energy. This proved a better system for temperature control than the 'sails' of *Dimetrodon* and *Edaphosaurus* and was adapted by their successors. These were the therapsids, and there is some evidence that certain of their advanced forms were warm-blooded. The therapsids showed improvements on the pelycosaurs, as their skull and body skeleton were adapted to a more active life. Specialization of the teeth continued, and in many forms the skull structure, coupled with larger jaw muscles, suggests that later therapsids could chew their food thoroughly. Early therapsids tended to sprawl, but in time changes in the arrangement of their limbs, hips and shoulders gave creatures such as *Lycaenops* and *Thrinaxodon* a much improved posture. According to some experts, *Thrinaxodon* had whisker pits on its snout, and if this is true we can assume that this and later therapsids were hairy. Mammal-like reptiles dominated the reptile group for over 35 million years.

The archosaurs

Crocodiles and alligators have been described as 'a mere remnant' of a once-prolific group of diapsid reptiles — the archosaurs. The word

Right: The duck-billed platypus belongs to the Monotremata, a group of egg-laying mammals. Included in this group are the spiny ant-eaters, and together these 2 creatures are regarded as comprising the most primitive mammalian order. Egg-laying is a reptilian characteristic and its persistence in the monotremes may serve as a clue to their ancestry. The monotremes are warm-blooded and have many other mammalian features.

Right: *Thrinaxodon* was a cynodont or 'dog-toothed' reptile from the Lower Triassic. It was about 450 mm long and was probably warm-blooded. Many of the lower jaw bones had been fused together, and large jaw muscles had developed to increase the animal's biting power.

Right: *Lycaenops* was a mammal-like reptile (therapsid) from the Upper Permian. It grew to just 1 metre in length and was more heavily built than the later cynodonts. The jaw structure was more advanced than that of the pelycosaurs and the teeth more varied in character. *Lycaenops* was a gorgonopian therapsid and it dominated Upper Permian communities.

Right: *Dimetrodon* and *Edaphosaurus* are the classic examples of sail-backed pelycosaurs. They flourished during the Lower Permian, when *Dimetrodon* was the major predator. The large fin was probably a device used to regulate temperature, and these pelycosaurs can be seen as an experimental stage in the development of warm-blooded creatures. The pelycosaurs and more advanced therapsids have similar skulls and teeth.

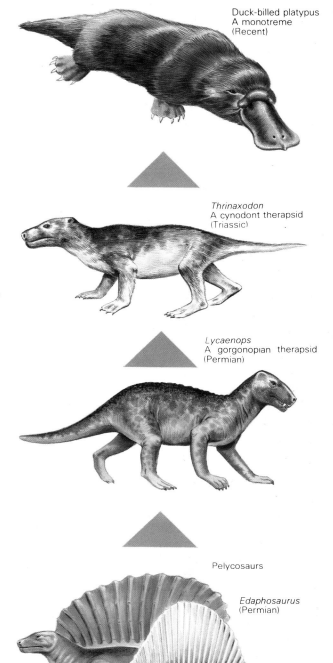

Duck-billed platypus
A monotreme
(Recent)

Thrinaxodon
A cynodont therapsid
(Triassic)

Lycaenops
A gorgonopian therapsid
(Permian)

Pelycosaurs

Edaphosaurus
(Permian)

Dimetrodon
(Permian)

L **Labyrinthodonts** were the major amphibians during the late Palaeozoic to early Mesozoic. They were

Mole, an insectivore

characterized by the labyrinthine structure of their teeth and by the development of ARCH VERTEBRAE. Many labyrinthodonts grew to a huge size and a number of groups adapted to a life on land. See also SEYMOURIAMORPHS.
Lampreys are living jawless fishes, or AGNATHANS. They have no scales and their eel-like bodies lack paired fins. Lampreys lead a SEMI-PARASITIC existence, attached to other fishes.
Larval describes a young developing animal that has to fend for itself. A typical larva is the tadpole of the

frog, which has external feathery gills and a large, broad tail. Larval stages exist in many invertebrates, including the echinoderms and brachiopods. Significant changes must take place before a larva can attain the adult form.
Leiopelmatids are living frogs, generally considered as rather primitive. They have more neck and back vertebrae than other living frogs and toads. The tadpole stage is also characteristic. Leiopelmatids range from the Jurassic to Recent periods.

Lepospondyls were a group of amphibians that lived during the late Palaeozoic. Most were of modest size and many became snake-like in appearance. They are characterized by HUSK VERTEBRAE.
Lesothosaurus was a small, BIRD-HIPPED dinosaur from the Upper Triassic of southern Africa. It lived at the same time as did HETERODONTOSAURUS and was about the same size. But *Lesothosaurus* had rather simple teeth and no muscular cheeks. Its head was also smaller, although it was

agile, and ran on its strong back legs.
Lithographic limestone is a fine-grained, compact sediment. By far the best-known example is that of Solnhofen in Bavaria, West Germany, which is made up of microscopic organisms and contains very well-preserved molluscs, fish and reptiles. Among the reptiles is the dinosaur *Compsognathus*, a small, agile COELUROSAUR. But most famous of all are the remains of *Archaeopteryx*, the first bird.
Litopterns are an extinct ORDER of South American

'archosaur' means 'ruling reptile' and aptly describes a group that includes the crocodiles and alligators, dinosaurs, PTEROSAURS and their common ancestors the THECODONTIANS.

The thecodontians, or 'tooth in socket reptiles', first appeared at the base of the Triassic (225 million years ago). At first the group contained clumsy 'sprawlers' such as *Chasmatosaurus*, whose legs splayed out sideways, but in time they were replaced by animals which held their bodies off the ground in what is called a 'semi-improved' posture. This involved changes in the shape and position of the limb bones and their movement with the shoulder and hip girdles. The legs were thus drawn closer to the body and thecodontians such as *Mandasuchus* and the two-legged *Euparkeria* could move over the ground in a faster, more efficient, manner. Some experts believe that a few thecodontians even attained the 'fully-improved' posture, with the limbs drawn beneath the body as in the higher mammals. Others doubt this, and claim that the 'fully-improved' stance is one of the essential differences between the thecodontians and their descendants — the dinosaurs. The 'improved' thecodontian limbs helped them to become dominant in the Middle Triassic; their explosive evolution was arrested only by the appearance of the 'terrible-lizards' (DINOSAURIA).

Competition among thecodontians themselves was intense during the Middle Triassic, and two groups, the AËTOSAURS and PHYTOSAURS successfully filled new ECOLOGICAL NICHES. The aëtosaurs grew heavy armour and specialized to a vegetarian or possibly OMNIVORE diet. They lived on land, but in common with the large crocodile-like phytosaurs they kept a primitive sprawling walk. Both groups were comparatively short-lived; they died out well before the end of the Triassic and the disappearance of their 'normal' thecodontian cousins.

SELECTION PRESSURES among competing thecodontians also led to the evolution of the pterosaurs and crocodiles, as well as the dinosaurs. Each stock inherited advantageous characters from their different ancestors, and further developments helped them to colonize new ecological niches. Crocodiles replaced the phytosaurs to become the chief flesh-eaters of rivers and river banks, with one group, the geosaurs, adapting to a sea-going life. Crocodiles survive to the present day, whereas their flying

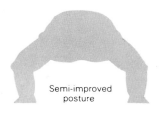

Below: In many thecodontians the limbs are drawn close to the body. This arrangement has the advantage of lifting the animal higher and enables it to move more easily, using less energy. This 'semi-improved' posture is found today in the living crocodiles and alligators.

Semi-improved posture

Phytosaurs

Rutiodon

Thecodontians

Ornithosuchus

Proterosuchus

Right: *Proterosuchus* and many early reptiles were rather slow-moving creatures. The upper arm was moved sideways and the forearm held vertically. This restricted the animals to a 'sprawling' gait.

Sprawling gait

UNGULATES. Descended from the CONDYLARTHS, litopterns developed horse- and camel-like forms.
Lizard-hipped dinosaurs, or saurischians, are those in which the pubis bone points downwards and forwards and the ischium bone downwards and backwards. This results in a 4-pronged arrangement of the pelvis, similar to the condition found in many other types of reptile. See also BIRD-HIPPED.
Lophodont cheek-teeth have rows of cusps fused into ridges. They are typical of BROWSERS.

Loxomma was a primitive amphibian from the Carboniferous. Like its relative *Megalocephalus* it was distributed over large areas and was characterized by keyhole-shaped eye-holes, which possibly held a facial gland as well as the eye itself. *Loxomma* and its rela-

Lions, like all mammals, are warm-blooded

tives had high yet narrow skulls and numerous large pointed teeth. These were similar in structure to those of TASSEL-FINNED fishes, while the vertebrae were more advanced in form than those of *Ichthyostega* and its relatives.

M **Mammals** are a class of VERTEBRATE animals. They are warm-blooded, have a protective or insulating cover of hair, and give birth to live young, which are suckled by the mother. MONOTREMES, however, lay eggs and in several other

ways display similarities to reptiles.
Mammoths were elephants adapted to living in cold environments. They were protected by a layer of fat and a coat of yellow wool covered by dark-brown hair. Their great curved tusks cleared away snow covering the grass on which they fed.
Marine turtles, such as the living green turtle and leathery turtle, are sea-going representatives of the tortoises, terrapins and turtles. They have flattened shells and large paddle- or flipper-shaped limbs. Of these, the

Below: Dinosaurs, mammal-like reptiles and mammals have their limbs drawn up beneath the body. This is caused by changes in the positions of their limb and girdle bones, and in the muscles. This 'fully-improved' posture separates dinosaurs from their thecodontian ancestors.

Fully-improved posture

Parasaurolophus

Crocodiles

Ornithischians

Diplodocus

Saurischians

Pterosaurs

Pteranodon

Desmatosuchus

cousins, the pterosaurs, died out at the end of the Cretaceous.

Dinosaurs appear

By the Middle Triassic dinosaurs had appeared in the southern continents. Though few in number they included both small BIPEDAL and large QUADRUPEDAL forms. They had attained the 'fully-improved' posture, and the two basic body designs seem to be adaptations enabling them to resist the pressures of the voracious thecodontians. Among the new two-legged archosaurs the BIRD-HIPPED dinosaurs, or ornithischians, were vegetarians. They were also fast runners and their appearance may have encouraged the development of similarly built meat-eaters. Like the large quadrupeds, the meat-eaters belonged to the saurischian or LIZARD-HIPPED dinosaurs and both probably shared the same ancestor.

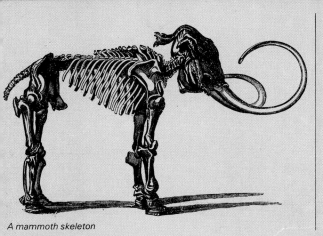

A mammoth skeleton

forelimbs are much the larger, and pull the animal through the water with a powerful 'flying' motion. Marine turtles first appeared in the Jurassic. The largest recorded genus to live in the sea is *Archelon,* which grew over 3.5 metres long.

Marsupials are MAMMALS that give birth to very small young which either crawl into the mother's pouch or cling to the mother's fur.

Mastodontosaurus is the largest known LABYRINTHO-DONT amphibian. Its skull alone measured over 1 metre in length, being broad and flat and noted for several tusk-like front teeth. Various species are recorded from Triassic rocks of Germany and India. *Mastodontosaurus* is associated with a group of labyrinthodonts called STEREOSPONDYLS, characterized by a flattening of the skull and an increased hardening of the vertebrae.

Mayomyzon is the only known fossil lamprey. It is therefore related to the CEPHALASPID fishes and is grouped together with the living form *Lampetra*. *Mayomyzon* grew to about 65 mm long. Like the living lamprey it had an eel-like body with long upper and lower limbs. Its mouth was narrow and slit-like, and it probably had a long, rasping tongue. Fossils of *Mayomyzon* occur as dark stains on the surface of Carboniferous sediments, with enough detail to recognize parts of the skeleton, gill pouches, the liver and gut.

Megalocephalus, like LOX-OMMA, was a LABYRINTHODONT amphibian. It was widespread during the Carboniferous, when it lived on the edges of the coal swamps. It had a large head,

This was once thought to be true for all dinosaurs, but the theory now is that ornithischians and saurischians were different types of archosaurs which evolved separately from different thecodontian lines.

Dinosaurs

During the Upper Triassic the evolution of the dinosaurs took on a fresh impetus and gradually they proved too competitive for their thecodontian ancestors. Small COELUROSAURS, large CARNOSAURS and even larger PROSAUROPODS were common and had spread over a wide area. As lizard-hipped dinosaurs they seem to be primitive types, but they were clearly more diverse than bird-hipped kinds. The coelurosaurs resembled their immediate ancestors and groups such as PROCOMPSOGNATHUS and COELOPHYSIS could easily have passed for thecodontians. Both were flesh-eaters and *Coelophysis* may even have been a cannibal. Carnosaurs were meat-eaters too, but they had already developed into large, heavily-built bipeds with sizeable dagger-like teeth. In contrast the prosauropods had four legs — a basic design which was continued by the gigantic SAUROPODS of the Jurassic and Cretaceous. The actual link between prosauropods and sauropods is in doubt, although MELANOROSAURUS from the Upper Triassic of South Africa seems an ideal ancestor.

No prosauropods survived into the Jurassic and so far as time is concerned they must be seen as one of the least successful dinosaur stocks. Increased size together with other advantages must have favoured the sauropods — for like the coelurosaurs, carnosaurs and ornithischians, they ruled the world for about 130 million years. During that time the lizard-hipped groups followed several evolutionary trends, as carnosaurs and sauropods became the largest meat-eaters and vegetarians to roam the Earth. Increased size was not important in the coelurosaurs, but the appearance of bird-like ornithomimids and large-brained dromaeosaurids shows how varied the group was.

The few examples of ornithischians from the Upper Triassic suggest that they had yet to establish themselves in secure niches. Unlike the saurischians, all ornithischians were plant-eaters and so when advancing into new habitats they may have met with a fiercer challenge. For

Right and below: Of all the reptiles, the dinosaurs were perhaps the most varied. They ranged from the size of a chicken to monsters 30 metres long. Various families adapted to different ways of life, and this is reflected in the size and form of their bodies. The different animals illustrated indicate that there are at least 19 types of dinosaur, each of which could be assigned to a different family.

Prosauropod

Pachycephalosaur

Atlantosaur

Hadrosaur

Normal coelurosaur

Camarosaur

Psittacosaur

Ornithomimid

Heterodontosaur

Stegosaur

Deinonychid

Iguanodont

Ankylosaur

Normal carnosaur

Ouranosaur

Protoceratopid

Spinosaur

Hypsilophodont

Ceratopid

---

with the characteristic keyhole-shaped eyes that link it with *Loxomma* at a family level. The skull was robust, with several prominent teeth. As in many primitive amphibians, its skull was high and rather narrow.
Melanorosaurus was a huge PROSAUROPOD which lived in South Africa during the latter half of the Triassic. It was 4-legged, and adults grew to almost 12 metres in length. It looked similar to *Diplodocus* or *Brachiosaurus* but differences in the skeleton separate it from the sauropods proper. Accord-

ing to many experts, *Melanorosaurus* may have been the ancestor of the great 'beast-footed' creatures of the Jurassic and Cretaceous periods. *Melanorosaurus* was a close relative of *Plateosaurus*, which lived in Europe at the same time.
Merychippus was a 3-toed horse that lived from mid-Miocene to Lower Pliocene times. Although its HYPSODONT teeth suggest it ate a diet of grass, the fact that *Merychippus* was much bigger than earlier horses implies that such specialized

teeth would have been needed even for a diet of leaves.
Mesosaurs were a group of ANAPSID reptiles that adapted to an aquatic life during the late Carboniferous and early Permian. They are confined to South Africa and South America. Few mesosaurs grew beyond 750 mm in length, and they were all slimly-built. Their skulls were long and armed with numerous sharp, long teeth. The neck was long and powerful, and the sideways flattened tail was the main swimming organ. The hind

limbs were used for movement, and the smaller front limbs for steering. Little is known of the feeding habits of mesosaurs, but they may have eaten small freshwater crustaceans, using their teeth as 'strainers'.

Mesosaurs represent an early side branch from the main line of anapsid reptiles.
Miacids were early CARNIVORA, and mainly tree-dwellers.
Miohippus was a small 3-toed horse that lived in

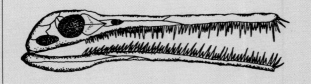

Mesosaurus

whereas the prosauropods found protection in marshy areas, small ornithischians such as LESOTHOSAURUS and HETERODONTOSAURUS lived in open, drier lands. To avoid predators they became fast runners, but during the Jurassic and Cretaceous several specialized groups evolved. These included the plated STEGOSAURS, armoured ANKYLOSAURS and horned CERATOPIANS — heavily-built and well-protected quadrupeds. The appearance of each marked periods of variation in ornithischian history. The greatest diversification happened in the Upper Cretaceous, when five major ornithischian families flourished. Among them were the ceratopians and ankylosaurs, but the two-legged hadrosaurs and PACHYCEPHALOSAURS were as important.

The evolution of the dinosaurs is therefore one of the great success stories of geological time. We can identify 19 or more different groupings and some experts say that their reign equalled 5,500,000 human generations. Why they survived for so long is difficult to answer; for instance it is hard to believe that the 'fully-improved' posture was such a major advantage. In recent years we have found evidence to suggest that the dinosaurs were warm-blooded. If proved, this would dismiss the belief that most dinosaurs were slow, cumbersome creatures. Warm blood need not have been essential for success, however, as the warm, equable Mesozoic climate was ideal for a group representing the peak of reptile evolution.

Below: The dinosaurs can be traced back into the early part of the Triassic period *(left)*. The first dinosaurs often resembled their thecodontian cousins, but within a short space of time, new and very different forms appeared throughout the world. The dinosaurs can be divided into 2 main branches by the different forms of their hip girdles *(right)*. The ornithischian (or bird-like) hip girdle, with the pubis bone extended beneath the ischium, appears more streamlined than the 4-pronged saurischian (or lizard-like) hip girdle.

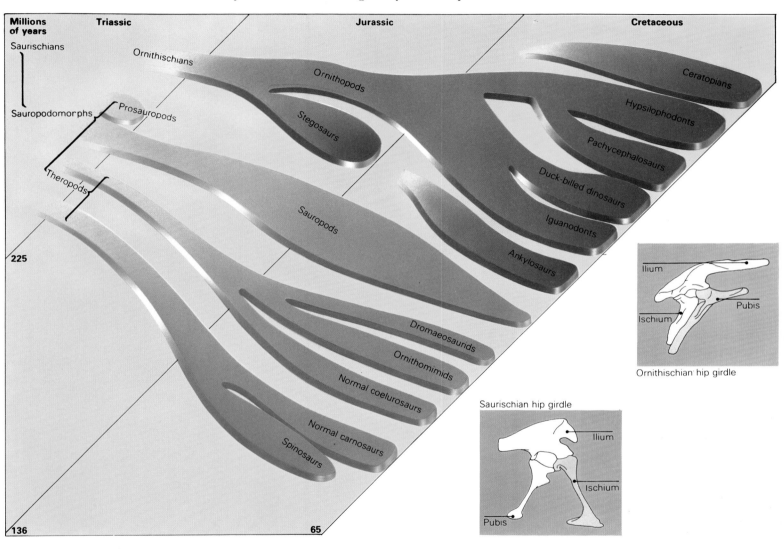

North America from mid-Oligocene to late Miocene times.
Molars are permanent cheek-teeth. HERBIVORES usually have complicated molars, whereas in the CARNIVORA they tend to be reduced.
Monotremes are an ORDER of primitive MAMMALS. They comprise the duck-billed platypus of Australia and the spiny ant-eating echidnas of Australia and New Guinea. They lay eggs, and have a body temperature which is lower than that of other mammals and also fluctu-

ates with the environment. In these respects monotremes are in transition from the reptiles, but approach the mammals as they have hair and suckle their young.
Mosaic evolution is shown in animals such as *Archaeopteryx* where an association of truly reptile characters and truly bird characters is found.
Mosasaurs lived only in Upper Cretaceous times, but were distributed worldwide. They are particularly common in the chalk rocks of Kansas, USA. Mosasaurs swam with snake-like move-

ments, and looked like the popular idea of a monster sea serpent.
Mud-grubbers refers to the mud-ingesting feeding

Mosasaurs looked like legendary sea monsters

habits of various animals without backbones and the ancient jawless fishes.
Multituberculates were probably the first herbivor-

ous mammals. They survived from the late Jurassic into the Eocene – a period of 100 million years – and are thus the longest-lived mammal ORDER ever.
Mustelidae are a family of the CARNIVORA which includes the weasels, skunks, otters and their kin.

N Neanderthal man was confined to western Europe, where he lived from about 80,000 to 35,000 years ago, during the early part of the last glaciation. Because he was shorter and much stockier than men today,

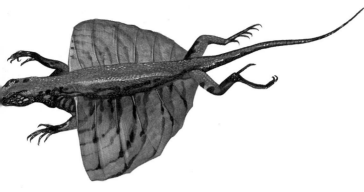

Left: *Kuhneosaurus* was one of the first flying vertebrates. It flourished during the Triassic, about 200 million years ago, in areas such as western England. In some ways it resembled the flying lizard *Draco* which lives in Asian rainforests.

Right: Primitive pterosaurs of the Jurassic, such as *Rhamphorhynchus,* had long tails and prominent, well-developed teeth.

Flying reptiles

During the Upper Permian and early Triassic, competition among reptiles forced some of the smaller creatures to take to the trees for protection. Specialization took place and reptiles capable of flight appeared. The first of these were the gliding lizards or KUHNEOSAURS, which had long hollow ribs covered by a strong membrane of skin. They fed on insects and probably caught their food while gliding to earth from the tree tops. However, they were really passive fliers, and true flight developed not in these gliding lizards but in a group descended from the thecodontians — the pterosaurs — the first of which is recorded from the Lower Jurassic.

The ancestry of the pterosaurs is shrouded by time but an ideal half-way group appears to be *Podopteryx.* This small Triassic reptile was also a glider, but unlike the kuhneosaurs had no extended ribs to support its two membranes. The first membrane ran between the front and back legs, and the second stretched from the back legs to the tail. As the forelimb grew longer, so the front membrane enlarged. This new state marked the appearance of the pterosaurs, or flying reptiles. The first was DIMORPHODON, which had a large, rather primitive skull and a long reptilian tail, like that of its close relative *Rhamphorhynchus.* These made up the more primitive group of pterosaurs and from them arose the more advanced PTERODACTYLOIDS. Their tail had all but vanished and the teeth were modified or even lost. *Pterodactylus* itself was the size of a sparrow but *Pteranodon* and *Quetzalcoatlus* had wing spans of 7 and 10 metres respectively.

Evolution of the birds

The first bird, ARCHAEOPTERYX ('ancient feath-

Right: *Pterodactylus* and its close relatives lacked the long reptilian tail of the rhamphorhynchoids. Most pterodactyloids also had modified, rather slender, teeth. They lived from the Upper Jurassic to Lower Cretaceous.

Below: The skeleton of *Pteranodon* shows clearly the dramatic elongation of the fourth finger to form a wing, and the strong development of the breastplate.

Above: *Pteranodon,* of the Upper Cretaceous, was one of the largest of all pterosaurs. Adults had a wingspan of over 7 metres, and their huge, bony crests were important stabilizers during flight.

New World monkey

Neanderthal man was once thought of as a separate species, but now he is widely accepted as a subspecies – *Homo sapiens neanderthalensis.*
Neural arch is the ⅄-shaped element that occurs above the central disc (centrum) of individual vertebrae (backbones). The arch is formed by 2 separate bony units and it covers the sides and upper surface of the spinal nerve cord. A prominent neural spine is found in many VERTEBRATES as an extension of the neural arch.
New World monkeys

(platyrrhines) differ from the Old World monkeys (catarrhines) especially in their nostrils, which open to the side rather than down, and because most have a tail with which they can grasp branches.
Newts have short legs and long bodies and are closely related to the SALAMANDERS. The majority of modern species exist in Europe, where they live close to water in which they lay their eggs. During the mating season many male newts develop crests.
Nothosaurs were a group

of primitive aquatic reptiles (EURYAPSIDS) that lived during the Triassic. They looked a little like small PLESIOSAURS.
Notochord is a slim rod of jelly-like material surrounded by a tough sheath found in animals such as AMPHIOXUS and a number of primitive VERTEBRATES. The notochord provides support, and is firm but flexible.
Notoungulates are an extinct and varied ORDER of mainly hoofed animals. They probably came from the CONDYLARTHS and with early exceptions were restricted to South America.

O **Old World monkeys,** see NEW WORLD MONKEYS.
Omnivore is an animal that eats a diet of both plants and animals.
Ophiderpeton, like SAUROPLEURA, was a snake-like LEPOSPONDYL from the Upper Carboniferous. It grew to just under 1 metre long and all vestiges of both front and hind limbs had disappeared. *Ophiderpeton* and its relatives *Phlegethontia* and *Dolichosoma* constitute a group of specialized lepospondyls which had forked single-headed ribs. Up to 200 vertebrae have been re-

er'), is recorded from the Upper Jurassic LITHOGRAPHIC LIMESTONE of Solnhofen in Bavaria, southern Germany. Of the five known specimens, three are incredibly well preserved and various parts of their skeleton show an ancestral link with the coelurosaurs. Feathers and differences in the hip and front limb, however, divide *Archaeopteryx* from its contemporaries such as *Compsognathus*. In many ways old 'ancient feather' is the classic example of MOSAIC EVOLUTION. Some characters remain distinctly reptilian, while others are definitely bird-like.

For some time after *Archaeopteryx* the fossil

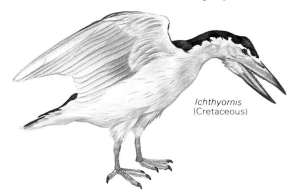

Ichthyornis
(Cretaceous)

history of the birds is poor. There is evidence in the Lower Cretaceous of goose-like and grebe-like birds, and a few bones to indicate that the 'fish-bird' ICHTHYORNIS had already appeared. This looked like the modern tern and in contrast to *Archaeopteryx* was an active flier. *Ichthyornis* was important among the Upper Cretaceous birds, and both it and its contemporaries BAPTORNIS and HESPERORNIS were fish-eaters with diver-like habits. *Hesperornis* was a large flightless bird, which like *Archaeopteryx* kept some reptilian characters, including teeth.

By the early Tertiary (65 million years ago) land and sea birds existed in several regions. Those living on land included ancestors of game-birds, waders, herons, and pigeons, while early relatives of the cormorants and petrels existed among sea birds. In Europe and North America a group of gigantic flightless birds, the DIATRY-MIFORMES ('terror-cranes') were the chief meat-eaters on land. One species, *Diatryma steini*, stood 2 metres high and its strongly-built legs indicate that it was a powerful runner. The 'terror-cranes' were a short-lived group; during the Oligocene EPOCH their place as major predators was taken

Above left and below: Two early bird forms. *Ichthyornis,* the tern-like 'fish-bird', lived during the latter half of the Cretaceous period. It flew well and probably ate fish. In the early Cainozoic the 'terror-cranes', or diatrymiformes, became the dominant bird group. They were flightless land-dwellers which grew exceptionally large.

Diatryma
(Eocene)

Owl
(Pleistocene)

Above: The so-called 'London *Archaeopteryx*' was found in 1861 near Pappenheim in southern Germany and was later bought by the British Museum for £700.

Left: Some experts claim that owls appeared in the Upper Cretaceous. Others suggest they began in the Cainozoic. They were common in Pleistocene bird groups.

by the fast-running PHORORHACIDS.

GIGANTISM in birds was common in the Middle and Upper Tertiary; for example, *Pachydyptes*, a penguin from the Oligocene of Australia and Antarctica, stood 1.5 metres high. The first owls, hawks and primitive swifts all appeared in the Oligocene and by the end of that epoch, modern groups accounted for almost 75 per cent of the world's bird life. Most living families had appeared by the start of the Pleistocene.

The rise of mammals

The Cainozoic, which opened about 65 million years ago, is often called the 'Age of MAMMALS'.

---

corded in these snake-like creatures. Each genus exhibited differences in the number and form of teeth, and it is likely that they fed on different organisms.
Order is a category used to classify plants and animals. An order is made up of related families; related orders make up a class. So among mammals, the classification for a timber wolf would be: class, Mammalia; order, Carnivora; family, CANIDAE; genus, *Canis*; species, *Canis lupus*; sub-species, *Canis lupus griseus*.
Oreodonts are extinct

A rat is omnivorous

North American ARTIODACTY-LA that lived from late Eocene until Pliocene times. They were somewhat pig-like, though as their teeth were SELENODONT they seem to have been RUMINANTS.
Osteichthyes are the higher bony fishes. They include both the RAY-FINNED and TASSEL-FINNED fishes.
Ostracoderms were those early AGNATHAN, or jawless, fishes that had a thick bony skeleton.
Otariidae are the eared seals and include fur seals and sea lions. Like the PHOCIDAE they can be traced

back to the Miocene.
Otic notch is found in higher vertebrates such as the amphibians and reptiles. It occurs at the back of the skull, and in early representatives of the reptiles and amphibians marked the site of the ear.
Oxyaenids were a family of the extinct CREODONTS and the most powerful predators of their times. They arose in the Palaeocene but died out at the end of the Eocene.

P **Pachycephalosaurs,** see BONE-HEADED.
Pachydyptes was a giant

penguin that lived during the Oligocene. Like all penguins it was a mixture of primitive and advanced features, the wings being modified to act as flippers. Flight was impossible with these, and the adaptation of the penguins to an aquatic life is also reflected in the webbed feet of its hind limbs. The penguins probably derived from strong-flying seabirds such as the albatross and petrel. *Pachydyptes* and several of its close relatives grew to the size of a man, and numerous species inhabited the coastal regions of Patagonia, Au-

Carnivora
(carnivores)

Creodonta

Cetacea
(whales, dolphins)

Taeniodontia

Tubilidentata
(aardvarks)

Tillodontia

Cretaceous
65

Artiodactyla
(even-toed ungulates)

Condylarthra

Perissodactyla
(odd-toed ungulates)

Litopterna

Notoungulata

Amblypoda

Palaeocene and Eocene
37.5

Astrapotheria

Oligocene – Pliocene
1.6

Hyracoidea
(hyraxes)

Pleistocene – Recent

Insectivora
(insect-eating mammals)

Chiroptera
(bats)

Dermoptera
(gliding lemurs)

Primates

Rodentia
(rodents)

Lagomorpha
(rabbits, hares)

Edentata
(sloths, anteaters)

Pholidota
(pangolins)

Multituberculata

Embrithopoda

Marsupialia
(pouched mammals)

Monotremata
(egg-laying mammals)

Desmostylia

Proboscidea
(elephants)

Sirenia
(dugongs, manatees)

Left: The adaptive radiation of the mammals established many different orders, or groups which share certain common adaptive traits. Several of the orders were established in the Mesozoic, but the majority arose during the early Tertiary, after the extinction of the dinosaurs. Some of the less advanced groups became extinct by the end of the Eocene, although other groups lived on into later Tertiary times and some did not finally disappear until the close of the Pliocene, especially in South America. A number of the surviving orders are evidently greatly reduced in variety compared with their diversity earlier in the Cainozoic era.

---

stralasia and Antarctica during the Tertiary period.
Palaeoniscid fishes are a primitive group of RAY-FINNED fishes from the Palaeozoic and early Mesozoic. Most were modest in size, and many resembled the living herring. But the palaeoniscids had shiny, thick, heavy scales. Many palaeoniscids had a HETEROCERCAL tail, large eyes and an elongated mouth. A typical example was *Cheirolepis* from the Devonian.
Palaeontologists study the geological periods of the past, and the forms of life

which existed within them.
Pantotheres are generally accepted as the ancestors of the higher mammals, based on the arrangement and working of their MOLARS.
Pecorans include deer, giraffes and the BOVOIDS, although sometimes the TRA-GULOIDS are included as well.
Pelycosaurs were a group of early SYNAPSID reptiles characterized, in several cases, by large dorsal (back) fins. They lived during the Permian, and both meat-and plant-eaters are known.
Perissodactyla are hoofed animals with an odd number

of toes. They have an excellent fossil history, which shows that they were once far more diverse.
Phocidae are earless or common seals, which first appear in the fossil record in Miocene rocks.
Phororhacids were a group of giant birds recorded from the Oligocene, Miocene and Pliocene epochs. *Phororhacos*, the best-known of these flightless animals, was long-legged and between 1.5 and 1.8 metres in height. It had a powerful beak and was possibly the major predator in

parts of South America. The phororhacids' success was probably linked with the ab-

Common seal

sence of PLACENTAL mammals from this region during the epochs in question.
Phytosaurs are among the most common THECODON-TIANS recorded from the Upper Triassic. They were advanced creatures whose general appearance was similar to that of living crocodiles. Like the AËTOSAURS, however, they were more heavily ar-moured than their contem-porary thecodontians or the crocodiles. A typical phy-tosaur, such as *Rutiodon*, had a long skull and strong jaws armed with numerous

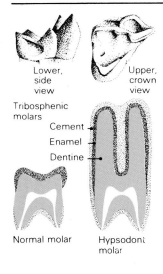

Lower, side view

Upper, crown view

Tribosphenic molars

Cement
Enamel
Dentine

Normal molar

Hypsodont molar

Hypsodont molar, crown view

Cement
Enamel
Dentine

Carnassial molars

Cat

Dog

Above: Fossil teeth are important in tracing evolutionary trends in mammals. Some early species had tribosphenic molar teeth that were used to cut and crush insects. In later mammals teeth became more specialized. Certain herbivores developed high-crowned or hypsodont molars, which, as they were used, developed ridges that were ideal for grinding. Carnivores developed carnassials for cutting and slicing meat. The carnassials shown are upper ones, with roots uppermost.

Yet mammals actually appeared around 100 million years earlier, in late Triassic times. They evolved from predatory therapsid reptiles (*see page 47*), and by the Jurassic had divided into five separate ORDERS of small, relatively insignificant animals. Of these, only the MULTI-TUBERCULATES, a group of pseudo-rodents, survived into the Cainozoic. The TRICONODONTS, SYMMETRODONTS and DOCODONTS were probably insect- or meat-eaters, and disappeared in the Jurassic or early Cretaceous. However, it may be that the docodonts were ancestors of the MONOTREMES which live in Australia and South-East Asia. The fifth order, the PANTOTHERES, also died out in the Cretaceous. These shrew-like creatures were INSECTIVOROUS and laid eggs, and from them arose the first PLACENTAL and MARSU-PIAL mammals. These two new evolutionary lines are recognized from fossils of their teeth, which even then were distinctly different.

The early marsupial *Eodelphis* was very like the living American opossum *Didelphis*, and later developed several types which flourished in the Cainozoic, especially in Australia and the Americas. Like their predecessors, the first placental mammals fed on insects. Before the Cretaceous ended they had given rise to several new orders, the most important being the CONDYLARTHS, CREODONTS and PRIMATES. Condylarths were primitive hoofed animals and seem to have been omnivorous. The creodonts, however, were meat-eaters, appearing before, and later evolving quite separately from, the true CARNI-VORES. The primates, of course, include man. Despite this diversity, mammals remained unimportant in both variety and size compared with the dinosaurs of the period.

At the start of the Cainozoic mammals underwent a spectacular burst of ADAPTIVE RADIATION to fill the places of meat- and plant-eating animals left empty after the dinosaurs died out. Old orders such as the multituberculates, creodonts and condylarths continued with great success, and at the same time began many new orders. Most modern and extinct herbivores, for example, are descended from the condylarths. And, although the origins are not always so clear as in this last case, it is likely that all the orders of mammals known only from the Cainozoic in fact extend back as far as the Palaeocene or Eocene.

Deteriorating climate and more competition among the rapidly evolving mammals led to many of the older, experimental forms declining or dying out in the late Eocene and Oligocene. The multituberculates were eliminated, along with the strange TAENIODONTS, TILLODONTS, AMBLYPODS and EMBRITHOPODS. Condylarths and DESMOSTYLIDS, on the other hand, survived into the Miocene, while the creodonts finally died out only in the Pliocene. As in the Miocene the geography of the world became more as it is today, so other mammal orders developed recognizable modern forms. These were perfected in the Pliocene, when the diversity of highly specialized mammals reached an all-time peak. Further adaptation took place during the Pleistocene ICE AGE, resulting in the mammals we see today. But these are far less varied than the mammals of the Pleistocene, for they were decimated by a wave of extinctions between 60,000 and 10,000 years ago. The larger mammals were particularly badly hit, and on each continent extinctions coincided with the spread of human hunters. The 'Age of Mammals' was over and the 'Age of Man' had begun.

While the main adaptive radiation of flowering plants happened before the continents drifted far apart, that of the mammals occurred afterwards. Since communication between the three northern continents was possible for much of the Cainozoic, their mammals are very similar and are almost all placental. This was not so in the three southern continents. Australian mammals are almost entirely marsupial, presumably because Australia was cut off before the m... highly evolved and competitive placental ma... mals could colonize it. Throughout the Tertiary in South America, marsupials also filled the flesh-eating and to a large extent the insect-eating niches. The herbivores were placental mammals, including such groups as the LITOP-TERNS, NOTOUNGULATES and ASTRAPOTHERES. This situation lasted until the end of the Pliocene, when the land connection between South and North America was re-established. Advanced placental mammals were then able to cross into South America, so causing the end of the native herbivores and marsupials, apart from the opossums. Africa has been less isolated than Australia and South America. So while it has characteristic mammals, there are no marsu-

---

sharp teeth. *Rutiodon* grew to over 6 metres, while its close relatives reached lengths up to 10 metres. Nostrils near the top of the skull probably allowed phytosaurs to breathe while most of the body was under water. Phytosaurs lived in swamps and by rivers. They fed on fish.
Pineal opening marks the position of the 'third eye' in fish, amphibians and certain reptiles. It is usually in the centre of the skull roof.
Pipids are a group of aquatic frogs. They lived from the Jurassic to Recent periods.

Placental mammals give birth to young which are at an advanced stage of development. Inside the mother they are fed through a placenta over a lengthy gestation period.
Placochelys was the most specialized of the PLACO-DONTS. In many ways it resembled a small MARINE TURTLE, for its body was covered with a thick shell. This was made up of hundreds of small plates similar to that of the living leathery turtle. *Placochelys* also had well-developed paddle-like limbs, but its skull was very differ-

Mammal feeding young

ent from a turtle's and the jaws were lined with robust crushing teeth. Sea turtles and the more specialized placodonts appear to be good examples of CONVER-GENT EVOLUTION.
Placoderms were one of the earliest groups of jawed fishes. Many were heavily armoured and members of the group are commonly referred to as 'plated-skins'.
Placodonts were a group of reptiles adapted to a life in water. The most advanced forms looked very much like large turtles and used their beak-like jaws to prise shell-

fish from the sea floor. They lived in the Triassic.
Plesiadapis was a tree-dwelling animal which resembled a squirrel, and had rodent-like teeth. True rodents may have evolved from plesiadapids.
Plesiosaurs are common in many Jurassic and Cretaceous rocks. They first appear in deposits which mark the changeover from the Triassic to Jurassic. By Liassic times they were already well diversified.
Pliohippus was a Pliocene horse of North America, one of several types that lived in

pials. In fact, the Pleistocene extinctions exaggerated the contrasts with the northern continents, for many animals now restricted to Africa once roamed widely outside it.

Hoofed mammals

Most hoofed mammals or UNGULATES belong either to the group with odd numbers of toes — PERISSODACTYLA — or to that with even numbers of toes — ARTIODACTYLA. Both are descended from the condylarths, but early perissodactyls differed from them in several ways. Their legs were longer, while their leg joints and small foot bones were developed to concentrate the thrust of their movement on to their central toes. Consequently the number of useful toes was gradually reduced to three or even one. Their cheek teeth also evolved in a distinctive way. The PRE-MOLARS became more like MOLARS, so increasing the area of grinding surface for crushing hard plants. These and other advances made the early odd-toed ungulates more efficient BROWSERS and faster runners than the condylarths, which they eventually eclipsed.

The initial radiation of the perissodactyls established the CERATOMORPHA, HIPPOMORPHA and ANCYLOPODA. Ceratomorphs include the rhinoceroses, primitive tapirs and some extinct groups closely related to the tapirs. Rhinoceroses and tapirs were once more varied; the hornless rhinoceros BALUCHITHERIUM, for instance, was the largest land mammal ever, and probably browsed tree-tops. The hippomorphs too are now much reduced. Only the horse and its allies survive, but once there were also massive TITANOTHERES standing over 2 metres high at the shoulder, and others like *Brontotherium* with Y- or V-shaped protuberances on their noses. There are no living ancylopods. The chief ones were the CHALICOTHERES, the more recent of which, such as *Moropus*, resembled clawed horses and survived until the late Pleistocene extinctions. Their claws were perhaps used to bend down leafy branches or to unearth roots and tubers.

Although various perissodactyls had already disappeared by the end of the Eocene and early Oligocene, the group reached its peak in mid-Tertiary times when the dominant ungulates were those with odd toes. They have since been displaced by the artiodactyls and seem headed

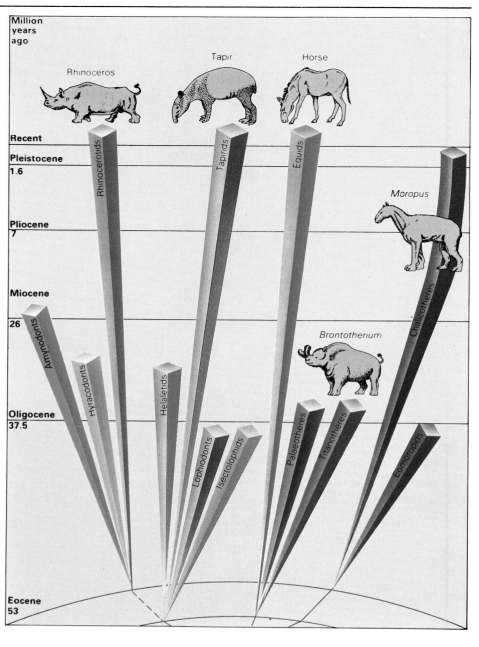

Above: The perissodactyls, or odd-toed ungulates, evolved in a way that established a variety of different families, and for a while they were the dominant ungulates. Many of the families became extinct in the Tertiary, and one was lost in the Pleistocene. The surviving families are much reduced in variety.

Left: These bones are from the hind foot of *Brontotherium.* A typical astragalus of a perissodactyl is also illustrated *(right),* showing the keeled upper surface for articulation with the tibia.

North America at that time.
Polypterus is a living bony fish of the RAY-FINNED type. It lives in fresh waters of tropical Africa. The body is covered in shiny, thick scales and its dorsal scale is modified to look like a series of small sails. *Polypterus* has retained a small pair of internal lungs which are of great value during droughts.
Predator is an animal that hunts and kills for its food. A typical example was *Tyrannosaurus.*
Prehistoric overkill is a term used to describe the impact of Palaeolithic (Old

Stone-age) hunters on the large mammals of the late Pleistocene. That hunting was responsible for the

Palaeolithic hunting tool

great Pleistocene extinctions is now widely accepted for some, if not all, of the continents.
Pre-molars are cheek-teeth which grow in front of the MOLARS.
Primates make up the ORDER to which man belongs.
Proboscideans are members of the ORDER Proboscidea; they include elephants and the extinct mastodons.
Procolophonids were an important group of STEM REPTILES. Some palaeontologists think they are ancestors of both the turtles

and the more advanced DIAPSIDS (such as dinosaurs and crocodiles).
Procompsognathus is a small COELUROSAUR recorded from sediments of the Upper Triassic. It was a lightly-built 2-legged animal, with thin-walled bones. Its head was small, with large eyes and a pointed snout. The neck was long and slender, and a long tail acted as a counterbalance during running. Adult procompsognathids reached 1 metre in length and the animal is known only from Europe. It is found in association with *Plateosaurus* — a

PROSAUROPOD — and the first turtle — *Triassochelys.*
Procyonidae are a family of the CARNIVORA, and include the raccoons, coatis and pandas. They spend much of their time in trees.
Prosauropods are a group of LIZARD-HIPPED dinosaurs from the middle and late Triassic. They were heavily-built, ate plants, and seem to be the ancestors of the giant SAUROPODS of the Jurassic and Cretaceous.
Prosimians are the least advanced PRIMATES. They include the lemurs, lorises and tarsiers. Lemurs survive

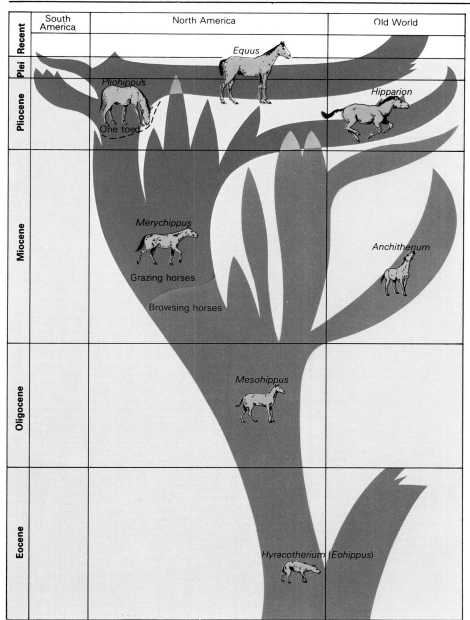

	South America	North America	Old World
Recent		*Equus*	
Plei			
Pliocene	*Pliohippus* One toed		*Hipparion*
Miocene		*Merychippus* Grazing horses Browsing horses	*Anchitherium*
Oligocene		*Mesohippus*	
Eocene		*Hyracotherium (Eohippus)*	

From 'Horses', Simpson (Oxford University Press)

Above: The modern family to which the horse, zebra and ass belong is the product of much evolutionary experiment. Although the majority of the advances occurred in North America, horses became extinct there in the Pleistocene and were reintroduced in the 1500s by the Spanish conquistadores. It can be seen that the modern horse is not the result of a single evolutionary development. It is instead the product of repeated trial and error. For example, the several types of browsing horses (those which lived off the leaves of trees and shrubs) became extinct in Miocene and Pliocene times. Most of the grazing horses, which lived off the grasslands of the world, disappeared in more recent times.

for extinction. All those living today are greatly reduced compared to their earlier geographical range, variety and numbers.

Adaptation in the horse

Evolutionary trends in perissodactyls can be seen in the development of the horse. The story is not of a single, progressive evolutionary line, but one of repeated trial and error. A move towards fewer toes began with the fox-sized *Hyracotherium,* or EOHIPPUS, which had miniature padded hooves. There were three toes on each hind foot and four on both front feet, although the fourth was largely useless. By the end of the Oligocene the sheep-sized MIOHIPPUS had three toes on each foot, and the central toe was further enlarged compared with that in *Hyracotherium.* Each toe was still functional and ended in a padded hoof. The first true plains horse, the pony-sized MERYCHIPPUS, also had three toes on each foot. But it walked only on the central toe, which ended in a hoof without a pad. In addition, the foot had developed a springing action. The earliest single-toed horse was PLIOHIPPUS, its side toes having been reduced to splints of bone in the upper foot. *Equus,* the modern horse, is a direct descendant of *Pliohippus.*

These adaptations for speed were accompanied by advances in horses' teeth. *Hyracotherium* had some molars with a bubbly surface on the crowns. This BUNODONT condition was well suited to an animal that browsed on the leaves of trees and bushes. Furthermore, the CANINES were smaller and a gap, or diastema, was left between them and the cheek teeth. Modern horses have large diastemas, which serve to collect food before it is passed backwards to the grinding teeth. In *Miohippus* the pre-molar teeth had become fully molar-like, with enamel ridges on the crowns. This LOPHODONT condition helped the animal to break down leaves with its teeth before digesting them. However, the crowns themselves remained low or BRACHYDONT. Cheek teeth equipped for grazing tougher grasses appeared in *Merychippus.* The crowns had increased in height to the HYPSODONT condition, were cement-covered, and the enamel ridges were folded into complex patterns. As the teeth wore down, the harder ridges stood above the softer cement and dentine in the cores of the teeth, so giving sharply crested grinding surfaces.

---

only in Madagascar, where there are no monkeys or apes to compete with. The lorises and tarsiers avoid such competition by being nocturnal.

Pterodactyloids were the most advanced group of PTEROSAURS. They appeared first during the Jurassic period and in contrast to the more primitive *Rhamphorhynchus* and *Dimorphodon,* had lost the long reptilian tail and possessed slender, delicate teeth. *Pterodactylus* itself was only the size of a sparrow whereas *Pteranodon* and *Quetzal-*

Lemur, a prosimian

coatlus were giants of the air. *Pteranodon* had a wingspan of 7 metres and *Quetzalcoatlus* one of 10 metres or more. In some pterodactyloids, such as *Dsungaripterus,* the jaws ended in long, sharp spikes and appear to have been used to spear fish. It is likely that *Dsungaripterus* and *Pteranodon* were ocean-going gliders whilst *Quetzalcoatlus* lived inland. There it soared over the plains like a great vulture searching for the carcass of dead animals.

Pterosaurs, or flying reptiles, arose in the early Jurassic, near salt water. They glided on air currents, for it is doubtful if they could have flapped their wing-like membranes. Probably they swooped over the sea to scoop up fish from the water. Their leg bones were arranged in such a way that they could not have stood upright on land.

Purgatorius is the earliest fossil primate and takes its name from the place where it was found—Purgatory Hill, Montana, USA.

Q **Quadrupedal** animals walk on 4 feet or legs.

R **Ramapithecus** differed from the Miocene apes or DRYOPITHECINES in having small CANINES and INCISORS, as in man, and a flatter face. Some authorities see *Ramapithecus* as an ape with HOMINID features; others believe it is the first, albeit primitive, hominid.

Ratfish are a group of opensea fishes which have a CARTILAGINOUS skeleton. They are therefore close relatives of the sharks and rays. Unlike their relatives they are quite rare, and their fossil record is limited. They are active swimmers, al-

Development of teeth and reduction of the toes did not always go together. HIPPARION was a contemporary of *Pliohippus,* and while its teeth were hypsodont it had three-toed feet.

Even-toed ungulates

In artiodactyls each foot generally has only four or two toes. These even-toed ungulates underwent an impressive radiation in the late Cainozoic, as the perissodactyls waned. There are various reasons for their success. For example they had, unlike the perissodactyls, an ankle-bone with grooves on the bottom as well as the top, and this is why artiodactyls are often able to make remarkable leaps. Again, many artiodactyls regurgitate their food for further chewing, after the risk of attack by predators is over. This adaptation, which permits hurried feeding but digestion at leisure, is known as rumination. The molar teeth of RUMINANTS have crescent-shaped or SELENODONT ridges, and in more advanced ruminants the upper incisors are replaced by a hard cropping pad.

The basic radiation of the artiodactyls happened in Eocene and early Oligocene times. Among the non-ruminants, the pigs and pec-

caries were defined at this early stage, as were the ANTHRACOTHERES — ancestors of the hippopotamus. Some early non-ruminant groups soon became extinct, however, including the ENTELODONTS, or giant pigs, the sheep-sized OREODONTS and the hare-like CAINOTHERES. Camels too appeared early, yet although these animals have a cropping pad and 'chew the cud' they are not usually classed as ruminants, because at the outset they were distinct from all other artiodactyls. The ruminants proper include the TRAGULOIDS (of which the chevrotains or mouse deer are the sole survivors) and the more advanced PECORANS. Deer evolved from the traguloids and in turn gave rise to the giraffes. BOVOIDS also branched from the traguloids, and diverged in the Pliocene into an astonishing array of animals — pronghorns, sheep, goats, musk-oxen, antelopes and cattle.

Below: Hind foot bones of a hippopotamus. Also shown *(right)* is a typical artiodactyl astragalus, with a double-pulley for articulation with the tibia and with the ankle bones.

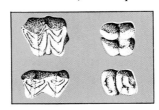
Left: Some artiodactyl teeth. Shown are those of a primitive Eocene artiodactyl *(right)* and the selenodont teeth of a Pleistocene antelope *(left).* Crown views are illustrated of worn left upper *(top)* and right lower molars *(bottom).*

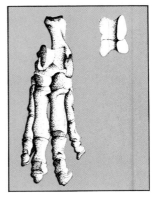

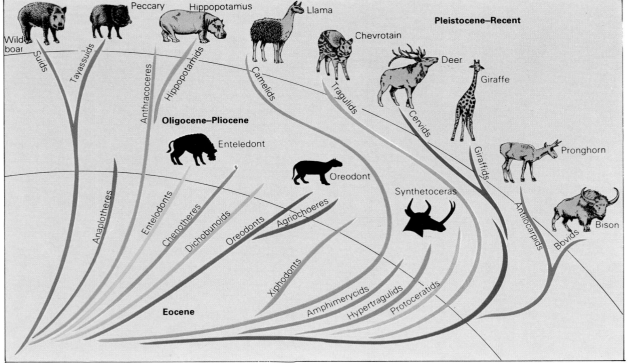

Left: The radiation of the artiodactyls, or even-toed ungulates, produced many different families, not all of which survived the Tertiary. They nonetheless remain the most varied and numerous ungulates.

though the tail is often reduced to a whip-like structure. Many forms have a long snout and a strange clasping organ is often found on the male's forehead. The ancestry of the ratfish may be traced back to the Devonian.
Ray-finned fishes constitute one of the 2 major groups of bony fishes. They are also known as the actinopterygians and are represented today by such fishes as salmon and trout. Several long-lived groups such as the palaeoniscids flourished during the

Palaeozoic and Mesozoic eras.
Reptiles are higher VERTEBRATE animals which have a scaly skin and lay AMNIOTE eggs. The class is subdivided by the characteristics of the skull, and scientists recognize 4 major subgroups among reptiles:- ANAPSIDS; DIAPSIDS; EURYAPSIDS; and SYNAPSIDS.
Rhipidistians are an extinct group of TASSEL-FINNED fishes from which the amphibians diverged in Devonian times. They were hunter-killers and unique in having internal nostrils. The fins of various

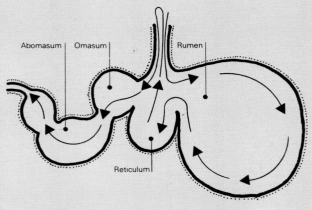
Ruminant's digestive system

rhipidistians have an arrangement of larger bones similar to the walking limbs of early amphibians.
Ruminants use a process whereby a pulpy mass of food is regurgitated from 2 stomach chambers — the rumen and reticulum — for chewing. After this it is swallowed again and passed into 2 other stomach chambers for further digestion.

S **Sabre-tooth cats,** see CANINES.
Salamander is the name given to the long-bodied, short-limbed members of

Palaeomastodon

Gnathabelodon

Gomphotherium

Indian elephant

Deinotherium

Woolly mammoth

The earliest undoubted PROBOSCIDEANS, *Palaeomastodon* and *Phiomia,* are known from the Lower Oligocene of Africa, where they probably evolved from condylarths which had migrated there. Both were elephant-like in appearance, *Phiomia,* the larger of the two, being about the size of a smallish modern elephant. By the Miocene three new groups had developed from them. The DEINOTHERES were hoe-tuskers, so called because they had powerful down-turned tusks on their lower jaws, which they presumably used for digging. Eventually the deinotheres grew to a height of almost 4 metres at the shoulder, yet otherwise they stayed remarkably unchanged until they disappeared in the wide-spread extinctions of large mammals at the end of the Pleistocene. The SHORT-JAWED MASTODONTS were a more varied group, essentially of browsers. They resembled modern elephants, but were shorter, stockier and had bunodont teeth. The last survived until perhaps as late as 6000 BC.

The third and last group were the GOM-PHOTHERES, or long-jawed mastodonts. At first they were just a larger version of *Phiomia,* but they later branched into a number of different evolutionary lines. One ended in the curious shovel-tuskers and spoonbill mastodonts, with highly specialized lower jaws. Another led to the first true elephants. These differ from mastodonts in having higher skulls, shorter jaws, and a taller, slimmer build. The key difference, however, is that elephants have high-crowned molar teeth with numerous enamel-covered cutting plates that are dentine-filled and cemented together. Developing such molars allowed the animals to change from browsing to grazing, and several kinds of elephant therefore evolved to make use of the grasslands. During the Pleistocene, straight-tusked elephants were common in the INTER-GLACIAL periods, and alternated with MAMMOTHS in the GLACIALS. One mammoth, *Elephas trogontherii,* was the largest proboscidean of all time, reaching about 4.5 metres at the shoulder. Although the later WOOLLY MAMMOTH was smaller, it was nevertheless an animal of

Above: A selection of extinct proboscideans and the living Indian elephant.

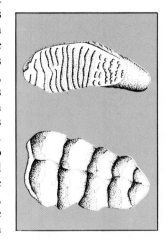

Above: The ridged upper molar tooth of a Pleistocene mammoth (*top*) is compared with the simpler upper molar of a Pleistocene mastodont (*bottom*).

Sabre-tooth cat jaw

the order Urodela. They are closely related to NEWTS but are perhaps nearer to the primitive amphibian condition. Today, many salamanders are adapted for a life on land, and lay their eggs in warm, damp areas. Most, however, prefer a life in water and breathe through gills throughout their lives. Living forms include the Mexican axolotl and the giant salamander from Japan. It is likely that the first salamanders appeared during the early part of the Mesozoic era. The oldest known salamander from the

Jurassic is similar to those of today.

Sauropleura is a snake-like LEPOSPONDYL amphibian recorded from the Carboniferous. The body is long, and apart from small vestiges the limbs have effectively disappeared. The skull is also long and pointed and appears to be adapted to an insect- or worm-eating diet. *Sauropleura* is also known as a nectridean, for its tail vertebrae have expanded fan-shaped neural spines (*see* NEURAL ARCH). *Sauropleura* and its close relative *Urocordylus,* which was also

snake-like, were abundant in the coal swamps, but only 1 or 2 nectrideans survived into the Permian period.

Sauropods were a group of LIZARD-HIPPED dinosaurs that flourished during the Jurassic and Cretaceous periods. The name means 'beast-footed' and this broad, elephantine foot was characteristic of PROSAUROPODS such as *Melanorosaurus* and sauropod dinosaurs such as *Brachiosaurus* and *Diplodocus.*

Scutosaurus roamed the late Permian landscape of today's USSR. It was a STEM

REPTILE and more specifically a representative of the pareiasaur family. The latter were the largest of the stem reptiles, characterized by the rotation of their limbs in towards the body. *Scutosaurus,* although not the largest pareiasaur, was almost 3 metres in length and had warty or horn-like protuberances on the face. Its limbs and backbone were massively built. *Scutosaurus* was a herbivore.

Selection pressures, such as competition for food, living space or shelter, have a considerable effect on

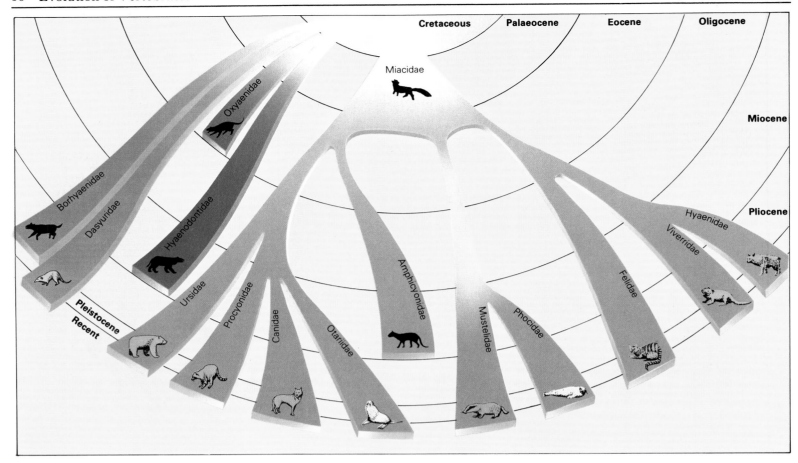

Above: Three quite separate orders of mammals have produced carnivores — the marsupials (red), the creodonts (blue) and the true Carnivora (green). The creodonts are extinct, as are the larger types of marsupial carnivores. The early Tertiary carnivorous mammals were so efficient and diverse that they prevented other lines of mammals from also becoming carnivorous.

impressive size. Only two species of elephant are living today; one in Africa and the other in India and South-East Asia. In effect, elephants, along with rhinoceroses, have been reduced to relic populations.

Flesh-eaters

Carnivorous mammals live by seeking and catching mostly vertebrate prey. They therefore evolved the senses, intelligence and the powerful, agile bodies needed for these tasks. Their teeth are also specially developed, with strong IN-CISORS for nipping, dagger-like canines for puncturing and stabbing, and blade-like cheek-teeth called CARNASSIALS which can be used for cutting up meat.

The earliest of the two placental types of carnivores — the creodonts — began in the Cretaceous. They later diversified into the cat-like OXYAENIDS and the HYAENODONTS. Hyaenod-onts included forms similar to the sabre-tooth,

dog, cat, and hyaena, and so foreshadowed many of the evolutionary lines that developed in the true CARNIVORA. Only the hyaenodonts survived the Eocene. They filled the role of scavengers until the end of the Miocene, when the ancestors of the modern hyaena displaced them. The oxyaenids died out early because the animals which formed their prey were evolving rapidly, and gradually a greater intelligence was needed to hunt them. As the Carnivora had larger brains, they succeeded where the creodonts had failed.

The carnivores living during the Palaeocene were weasel-like MIACIDS. They died out in the Eocene, but gave rise to the CANOIDEA and FELOIDEA. Of the canoids, dogs (CANIDAE) and the weasels and their allies (MUSTELIDAE) were living at the transition from the Eocene to the Oligocene. The weasel family later diversified widely and the otter part branched to give the seals (PHOCIDAE). Dogs did not become as highly

evolution. Successful competitors are obviously better adapted to the prevailing conditions and they will therefore pass on to their offspring the necessary information for success.

Selenodont teeth have highly developed crescent cusps, and are typical of RUMINANTS. So when they are found in fossil form it is assumed that the animals to which they belonged were also ruminants, but this is by no means certain (*see* OREO-DONTS).

Semi-aquatic animals spend much of their life in

Semi-aquatic mammal, an otter

water. Usually they are quite capable of existing on land, but competition and/or the need for protection leads to their occupying habitats on the margins of swamps and lake edges.

Semi-parasitic describes the way of life of an organism that obtains part of its food directly from another living animal or plant. The blood-sucking LAMPREYS are semi-parasites.

Seymouria is a medium-sized LABYRINTHODONT from the Lower Permian of Texas, North America, the skeleton of which exhibits a number

of amphibian and reptilian characteristics. Because of this, many palaeontologists believed that the animal and its close relatives were 'link fossils' which were the true ancestors of the REPTILES. *Seymouria* was 75 mm long, sturdily built, and seemingly adapted to a more terrestrial life than other amphibians.

Seymouriamorphs were a group of medium-sized LABY-RINTHODONT amphibians from the Permian period. They were among the most advanced forms of amphibian to walk on Earth and were specialized towards a land-

based way of life. It was once thought that they were the true ancestors of the reptiles, but this is now doubted as they appear too late in the fossil record.

Short-jawed mastodonts appeared in the Miocene, and some of them later came to resemble the great straight-tusked elephants of the Pleistocene.

Smilodon was a large sabre-tooth cat that lived in the New World from Upper Pliocene until late Pleistocene times. Although many people assume that it preyed upon slow-moving

Smilodon,
Upper Pliocene-Pleistocene

Thylacoleo, Pleistocene

Homotherium,
Upper Pliocene-Pleistocene

Thylacosmilus, Pliocene

the cats we know today — the most advanced land carnivores. Hyaenas (HYAENIDAE) are the youngest feloids, and evolved rapidly from the civets in the late Miocene.

Apart from the placental animals described above, meat-eaters also evolved among the marsupials. The wolf-like BORHYAENA roamed parts of South America in the Miocene, to be succeeded in the Pliocene by the larger sabre-tooth 'cat' THYLACOSMILUS. This animal showed a remarkable likeness to later placental American sabre-toothed cats, such as SMILODON, and provides a good example of CONVERGENT EVOLUTION. The extinct THYLACOLEO of Australia was once described as a marsupial 'lion', but we now seem to think it was a specialized herbivore! Even so, there are small native 'cats' in Australia, as well as the larger Tasmanian devil

Left: *Homotherium* and *Smilodon* were placental sabre-tooth cats. The sabres of *Homotherium* were extremely flattened and the animal preyed on young elephants. *Thylacosmilus* was a marsupial equivalent of the sabre-tooth cats, and it is possible also that *Thylacoleo* was a large lion-sized marsupial carnivore.

Below: The dog-bear *Hemicyon,* and the big dire wolf of the Pleistocene are just 2 of the many extinct relatives of the dogs. Also shown is the rather dog-like marsupial, known as *Borhyaena,* which lived in the Miocene of South America, as well as *Thylacinus,* the so-called Tasmanian 'wolf'.

specialized, which accounts for the fact that they are now the most widely-spread carnivores. But several new families broke away from the canids — the extinct dog-bears (AMPHICYONIDAE), sea lions (OTARIIDAE), raccoons and pandas (PROCYONIDAE) and, most recent of all, bears (URSIDAE). It is interesting that some of the raccoons and bears are omnivorous, while pandas are strictly vegetarian.

The Old World civets (VIVERRIDAE) are the most primitive feloids, being little-modified descendants of the Eocene miacids. By late Eocene times cats (FELIDAE) had separated from the miacids and were modern in their appearance by the early Oligocene. Two cat types then developed. First there were large, heavy SABRE-TOOTH CATS which preyed on slow-moving animals. They vanished at the end of the Pleistocene, together with the animals they hunted. The other cats were swifter and more agile, and so able to chase faster prey. These are

Canis dirus,
Pleistocene

Hemicyon (dog-bear)
Miocene- Pliocene

Borhyaena,
Miocene

Thylacinus, Pleistocene-Recent

mammals, *Smilodon* may have been a scavenger, using its fearsome CANINES to open and divide carcasses.
Stegosaurs were a group of plated dinosaurs. They were QUADRUPEDAL plant-eaters and are known from the Upper Jurassic of North America and Africa. *Stegosaurus* may have been able to control its body temperature by regulating the flow of blood into the large, bony plates set along its back.
Stem reptiles are those, other than the turtles, that have an ANAPSID skull. They

Subholostean link, Acipenser

are also known as the cotylosaurs and were, with the SYNAPSIDS, the prominent reptiles of the late Palaeozoic and early Mesozoic.
Stereospondyls were a group of amphibians alive during the Upper Permian and Triassic. They were represented by animals such as *Rhinesuchus.* Stereospondyls were more advanced than their *Eryops*-like ancestors. They had a flatter skull than *Eryops* and their vertebrae had a distinctive ring-shaped centre. This marks the stereospondylus type of ARCH VERTEBRAE.
Subholostean describes a group of RAY-FINNED fishes that flourished during the

early Mesozoic. In many ways they resemble the most primitive ray-fins – the PALAEONISCIDS – but several features (including a modification of the tail, fewer rays within the fins and thinner scales) indicate that they were more advanced. Included in the subholosteans are the deep-bodied *Dorypterus* and *Saurichthys* which resembles the freshwater pike. *Saurichthys* had a long body and its elongate mouth was lined with sharp teeth. Subholosteans are known from the Upper Carboniferous and are probably linked

with the living sturgeon *Acipenser.*
'Survival of the fittest' refers to the ability of organisms to compete against others and survive. Their success may result from some small, seemingly insignificant character which is then inherited by successive generations.
Symmetrodonts were primitive MAMMALS, and take their name from the fact that their MOLARS had 3 pointed cusps, which in the crown view are arranged in a symmetrical triangle, rather than in a straight line.

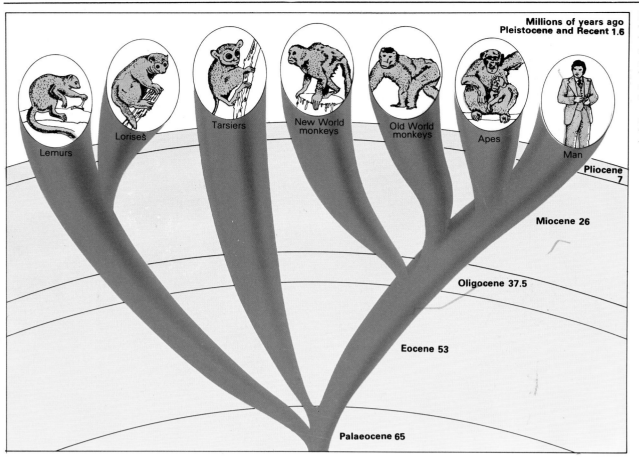

Millions of years ago
Pleistocene and Recent 1.6

Lemurs

Lorises

Tarsiers

New World monkeys

Old World monkeys

Apes

Man

Pliocene 7

Miocene 26

Oligocene 37.5

Eocene 53

Palaeocene 65

Left: The evolutionary 'tree' for the primates indicates that all the living forms have evolved separately from the ancestral stock. This means, for example, that the apes are not included in the evolutionary line that led to man. The forerunners of apes and men developed from an earlier common forebear.

and, if it still exists, the TASMANIAN WOLF or thylacine.

Primates

In the early Cainozoic primates became more fully adapted for a life in the trees. But as their bodies grew larger they could no longer walk along slender branches and twigs. Only by jumping or swinging from branch to branch could they move quickly through the tree-tops. This required longer, stronger arms, opposable first digits on the hands and feet, and nails to replace claws. Also, the eyes moved to the front of the head so as to give BINOCULAR VISION, which was vital in being able to judge distances to be jumped. Since a sense of smell was not very important to animals living in trees where they could eat insects and fruit, the primate nose and snout became smaller, resulting in a flatter face. Finally, a larger brain was also essential, for rapid co-ordination of movement and senses.

The earliest known primate, PURGATORIUS, arose from an ancestor similar to the tree-shrew in the late Cretaceous. By the mid-Palaeocene it had given rise to three new groups, typical of which was the squirrel-like PLESIADAPIS. They were in turn replaced in the Eocene by yet another three groups, which were without rodent-like characteristics and from which all modern primates descend. The PROSIMIANS, which include lemurs, lorises and tarsiers, were a separate group before the end of the Eocene. They are the most primitive primates, and lemurs, for example, still have longer legs than arms and a rather fox-like muzzle. The more advanced ANTHROPOIDS, to which monkeys, apes and men belong, appeared later. The OLD WORLD MONKEYS and NEW WORLD MONKEYS were certainly in existence by the Oligocene, and had diverged from the same stock. Forerunners of the apes appear in the Oligocene as well, apparently having a common origin with the monkeys.

Synapsid is the type of skull present in the PELYCOSAURS, mammal-like THERAPSIDS and mammals themselves. It is characterized by a single large opening on the temple at approximately the same level as the eye.

Taeniodonts are an extinct North American ORDER dating from the Palaeocene and Eocene. They were an offshoot of INSECTIVOROUS animals with grinding teeth that indicate a plant-eating way of life. Some taeniodont forms were like heavy dogs.

Tasmanian wolf is probably extinct. Once common in Australia, its last traces were found in Tasmania, where some hair and footprints from this dog-like

Tasmanian wolf

marsupial were discovered in the mid-1960s.

Tassel-finned fishes or crossopterygians are characterized by fleshy, lobed fins. They are represented today by the lungfishes and the coelacanth. Many palaeontologists believe that the group is closely linked with the evolution of amphibians.

Teleosts are the most successful group of living fishes. They are RAY-FINNED fishes and their internal skeleton is composed almost entirely of bone. The teleosts are very varied, the catfishes and seahorses representing lines of evolution outside those of the more typical salmon, trout and freshwater pike.

Tetrapod means '4-footed' and is a term used of the

higher groups of vertebrates (amphibians, reptiles and mammals).

Thecodontians were early, primitive ARCHOSAUR reptiles which are known to be the ancestors of the dinosaurs, crocodiles and PTEROSAURS. They lived from the Upper Permian to the Upper Triassic.

Therapsids were a major order of SYNAPSID reptiles. Various families reveal a gradual evolution towards the mammals. The therapsids are also known as the mammal-like reptiles or paramammals.

The Miocene DRYOPITHECINES were undoubtedly apes. From them evolved two different HOMINOID lines. One led to today's gibbons and great apes; the other began about 14 million years ago with RAMAPITHECUS. The teeth of *Ramapithecus* show a departure from a fruit and leaf diet. Combined effects of a larger body and a reduced area of forested land resulting from changes in climate probably forced *Ramapithecus* to forage on the ground for more varied foods. Without any other form of defence, *Ramapithecus* may have used sticks and stones to ward off attacking predators. Whether the animal was itself an ape or a HOMINID is debatable, but there is little question that it was in the direct line of descent to the first true men. These appeared in Africa at least 3 million years ago. Early types like HOMO HABILIS and AUSTRALOPITHECUS gave way to HOMO ERECTUS, the forebear of modern man (HOMO SAPIENS) and his NEANDERTHAL relatives.

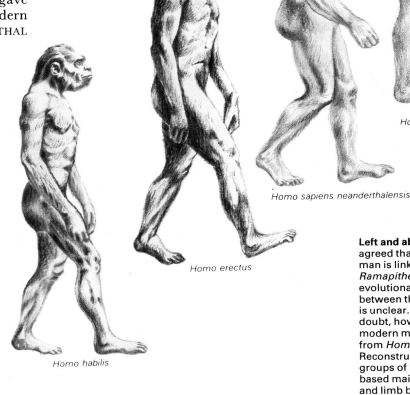

Homo sapiens sapiens

Homo sapiens neanderthalensis

Homo erectus

Homo habilis

Australopithecus

Ramapithecus

Left and above: While it is agreed that the family of man is linked to *Ramapithecus,* the precise evolutionary relationships between the early hominids is unclear. There seems little doubt, however, that modern men are descended from *Homo erectus*. Reconstructions of extinct groups of hominids are based mainly on fossil skulls and limb bones. From these it is often possible to estimate brain capacity, posture and movement. Evidence for the way of life of various early hominids is supplied by archaeological material found alongside their remains, and by the sediments in which they are preserved.

Thylacoleo was a lion-sized MARSUPIAL that roamed Australia during the Pleistocene. Its CARNASSIALS suggest that it was a CARNIVORE, but probably these shearing teeth were used to cut fruit.

Thylacosmilus was a South American MARSUPIAL which was as large as a tiger. It had enormously elongated, blade-like CANINES, and a deep flange of bone, the purpose of which was to protect these teeth in the lower jaw.

Tillodonts culminated in bear-sized, rodent-like animals in the Eocene and then died out.

Titanotheres were great beasts that stood over 2 metres high at the shoulder. Certain types, like *Brontotherium*, had Y- or V-shaped protuberances on their noses.

Traguloids are a superfamily of the ARTIODACTYLA and include the living tragulids, and the extinct hypertragulids, protoceratids and gelocids.

Triconodonts were primitive mammals whose fossils are identified by their MOLARS. Whereas most reptile teeth were conical or peg-like and single-rooted, early mammals had a more complex arrangement. The cheek teeth bore cusps, and the triconodonts had 3 in line, the central one being the largest.

Tunicates are marine animals that look like sponges. They have no pores, however, and the shapeless form is covered by a leathery skin. Some tunicates float, but others live in colonies on the sea-floor. Their larvae are tadpole-like, and the possession of a NOTOCHORD indicates that these animals are related to both AMPHIOXUS and the VERTEBRATES. Some experts believe that larvae of some ancient tunicates reached sexual maturity before they changed into sac-like adults, and that these larvae gave rise to a more advanced free-swimming animal which was the forerunner of the fishes.

U Ungulates, or hoofed mammals, include almost all the larger plant-eating mammals.

Ursidae are members of the bear family. They first appeared in the Miocene and are unusual in the CARNIVORA

Panda

The influence of man

Towards the end of the last Ice Age (about 10,000 years ago), a wave of extinctions drastically reduced the variety of larger mammals on the different continents. In all roughly 200 genera disappeared. Disease and climatic change have been suggested as causes, but neither explanation is convincing. It seems most improbable that, even if stricken by disease, there were no immune individuals in the species concerned. As for possible climatic controls, it is true that there were major changes as glacial environments gave way to inter-glacial ones. Yet similar developments had happened repeatedly before in the Pleistocene without such adverse consequences. Moreover, the extinct camels and shasta sloths of North America should actually have benefited from the spread of arid lands.

An explanation which fits the facts better is that of PREHISTORIC OVERKILL. Nowhere do the main extinctions come before the spread of men with relatively advanced hunting techniques. In the scale and timing of losses, Africa and North America represent two extremes. In Africa the decline began about 60,000 years ago, with the development there of late ACHEULEAN hand-axe cultures. Around 30 per cent of Africa's mid-

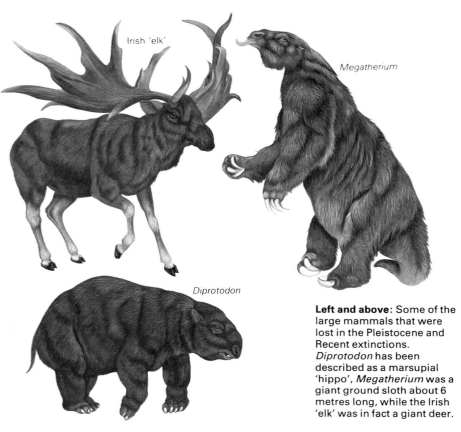

Left and above: Some of the large mammals that were lost in the Pleistocene and Recent extinctions. *Diprotodon* has been described as a marsupial 'hippo', *Megatherium* was a giant ground sloth about 6 metres long, while the Irish 'elk' was in fact a giant deer.

Left: Domesticated animals often look quite different from their wild ancestors, both in colour, size and shape. In this case, the domesticated pig *(below)* is longer than the wild boar *(above)*, from which it is descended, and has a pinkish instead of a black-brown coat. The extra length was bred for brawn and pork, while the loss of natural colouring is not important, since a domesticated animal does not need a camouflaged coat to help it avoid predators.

Pleistocene mammals vanished. In North America the decline began as recently as 11,000 years ago, and over the next 1,000 years nearly 70 per cent of North American mammals were eliminated! Again the decline coincided with the arrival in that continent of the first modern men. Extinctions on islands like Madagascar happened even later, well into historical times, for islands were the last places to be colonized by men.

Another feature which points to man's influence is that the animals which died out were without evolutionary replacements. The niches they occupied have not been filled, except by DOMESTICATED ANIMALS. Generally speaking, these are the only animals that have prospered since the Pleistocene, for the decrease in most wild animals continues. The need for GENETIC CONSERVATION is just one reason why some people view this loss with concern. Wild animals can provide genes for improving existing domesticated ones, as well as new candidates for domestication in the future.

---

in having a mixed or mainly plant diet. The giant panda is actually a primitive offshoot from the early bears.

V **Vertebrates** are, like graptolites and sea squirts, CHORDATE *(see page 26)* animals. Their essential characteristic is the possession of a strengthening rod of tissue, the NOTOCHORD. In the vertebrates the spinal cord is supported by a number of bony structures called vertebrae, and the notochord itself has been reduced, modified or lost.
Viverridae are a family

comprising the civets, genets, mongooses and their kin. They are mainly spotted or striped forest-dwellers.

W **Woolly mammoth** ranged over all the arctic lands of the northern hemisphere in the late Pleistocene. It probably lived on the tundra during the summer, and retreated to the woodlands farther south in the winter.

X **Xylacanthus** is a RAT-FISH from the Lower Devonian. It was a long-bodied,

lightly-armoured 'spiny-shark'. The body was probably covered with closely-fitting scales which had a

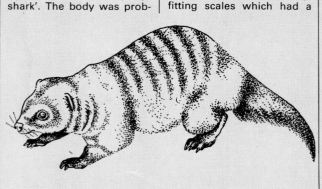

A mongoose

fitting scales which had a

concentric layered structure. The spines — 2 on the upper surface and several below — were probably long and pointed. The spiny-sharks ranged from the Silurian to the Carboniferous.

Index

Acknowledgements

Contributing artists
Ann Baum, Michael Bilsland, Jim Channell, Drury Lane Studios, John Gosler, Delyth Jones, Chris King, Tom McArthur, Jim Marks, Tony Morris, Peter North, Nigel Osborne, Michael Shoebridge, Ralph Stobart, Dorothy Tucker

The Publishers also wish to thank the following:
Heather Angel 10B, 12B, 18B, 19B, 21BL, 22B, 24B, 25B, 27B, 30B, 32B, 43T, 46B, 55B, 64CL, 68T B
Ardea/Peter Green 56B
Biophoto Associates 11B, 13B, 15BL BR
Bruce Coleman Ltd/Hans Reinhard 37T
Mary Evans Picture Library 7B, 8B, 14BL BR, 40B, 51B
Robert Harding Associates/Rainbird 37B
Imitor 3B, 4B, 16B, 21BR, 31B, 39B, 41B, 53T
Macdonald Educational/Kenya High Commission 48B
Mansell Collection 5B, 17B, 42B, 49B
Pat Morris 45B, 52B, 60B
Natural Science Photos/P.A. Bowman 47B
Natural Science Photos/G. Kinns 53B, 64TL
Natural Science Photos/Peter Ward 6B, 36B, 61B
Novosti 9B
Oxford Scientific Films/Kennedy 6TL
Oxford Scientific Films/Ziglesczynski 42T
R.I.D.A./David Bayliss 6TR, 11TC, 17TL TR, 23T
John Topham Picture Library 28B, 35B, 38B, 43B, 44B, 54B, 57B, 62B, 63B
John Topham Picture Library/Jane Burton 26B